Five Years of Bad Coffee

Five Years of Bad Coffee

✦

A White-Collar Criminal Does Blue-Collar Time

Nelson Christensen

iUniverse, Inc.
New York Lincoln Shanghai

Five Years of Bad Coffee
A White-Collar Criminal Does Blue-Collar Time

iUniverse books may be ordered through booksellers or by contacting:

iUniverse
2021 Pine Lake Road, Suite 100
Lincoln, NE 68512
www.iuniverse.com
1-800-Authors (1-800-288-4677)

ISBN-13: 978-0-595-37326-0 (pbk)
ISBN-13: 978-0-595-81724-5 (ebk)
ISBN-10: 0-595-37326-7 (pbk)
ISBN-10: 0-595-81724-6 (ebk)

Printed in the United States of America

Contents

Introduction

High school scholar, leader and athlete. Phi Beta Kappa and cum laude college graduate. Naval Officer on a three-star Admiral's staff at age 21. A 27-year career as a lawyer. Member of the Bar of the United States Supreme Court. Chairman of a major city Planning Commission. Father of three successful adult children. *Convict*!

My charmed life took a detour in 1995, when I confronted the fact that after nearly thirty years of the honorable practice of law, I had fallen into web of fraud and embezzlement, the consequence of having more money dropped into my lap than I had the character to handle. I had been negotiating and closing business deals in the Korean community in and around Seattle. Huge amounts of money would be placed with me, with no instructions other than to hold the money until I was told what to do with it. A subsequent audit of my trust account by the Bar Association showed that $23,000,000 went through my hands in a year and a half. Unfortunately, some of it stuck.

I was never caught. I decided on May 15, 1995 to pull the plug on my life of crime and face the consequences. What happened in the next three and a half years is another story. This book begins in 1998, when I submitted to the judicial process and was sentenced to five years in prison. I entered the prison system on November 2, 1998. I served 36 months in three different institutions, and was sent to work release for four months. Having earned a one-third reduction of my sentence for "good behavior" and "programming", I was released to freedom after forty months of confinement.

I served time in three prison facilities. The first, where we were sorted out for permanent assignments, was as hard and nasty as any prison that Cagney or Stallone endured in the movies. All levels of criminality were thrown in together...murders, drug dealers, forgers and run-of-the mill thieves like me. Next I went to a labor camp in the Olympic Rain Forest, at the absolute northwest corner of the United States, a hard work environment far from nowhere. After twenty months there, I requested and was granted a transfer to a prison dairy farm near home, where I herded 750 cows in all kinds of summer and winter weather. Finally, I went to five months of Work Release in Seattle.

I started to write about my experiences the first day I was in a high security cell at the Washington Corrections Center in Shelton, Washington. For many weeks, all I had to write with was a stubby golf scoring pencil. Later, I was able to get normal pencils and some ball point pens. Eventually, two and a half years later, I obtained a portable electric typewriter from another inmate through some clandestine actions involving a complex barter for food products.

The only thing that you have a lot of in prison is time. Time is the penalty, but time is also a gift. I read more and wrote more in those forty months than I did in my preceding 58 years of freedom. I filled many notebooks and legal pads with writing, and my letters to my friends and family were mostly saved by them. I had a vast amount of written material when I got home. However, I was not ready to confront it for several months. Finally, I got comfortable with it, and I started to edit it and put it on the computer.

Prison is in many ways not as bad as one expects, and in some ways it is worse. It was different for me, as a white 58-year-old professional with no prior record, than it was for many of my younger fellow inmates. In a strictly physical sense, prison is generally not dangerous or brutal. You *can* safely "drop the soap" (Just don't bend over to pick it up!) The guards usually do not beat you up, although sometimes they are so petty and bureaucratic that you might rather get hit in the mouth. Just like living in any big city, there are places where you should not go, and things you should not do. If you follow the rules and hang out with the better people, you get along. Of course, "better people" is a relative term when you are living in prison. It often includes murderers!

I did "good time", meaning that I made the best use I could of the considerable time that I had. Six hours a week in church, twelve hours in the weight room, regular meals—nutritious, if not always tasty—regular hours of sleep, and no booze, yield a very healthy person. Endless time for reading and writing, and funky libraries stocked with an eclectic variety of books, furnish an opportunity for great improvement of the mind. I had graduated from college and law school, but I got more of an education, from books and otherwise, in three years in prison than in all of my university years.

It was not, however, all a day at the beach. I got punched out a couple of times, just desserts for my smart-ass lawyer's mouth directed at the wrong persons. I have a nice scar over my left eye and a permanent lump above my lip as badges of my prison experience. I lived so far away from civilization for twenty months, in a forest labor camp in the Olympic Rain Forest, that I seldom had visitors. The day-after-day routine and ceaseless pettiness of prison life, and the isolation from loved ones who are graduating, getting married, celebrating anniversaries and holidays, and dying, and, for many inmates, the burning out of relationships, are the real punishment.

I had many good friends in prison, although not often people whom I would have chosen for friends on the outside, "on the streets", as we say inside. I have had virtually no contact with any of them since I got out. Nevertheless, in prison I shared common day-to-day interests with men of many races, often far younger than me and with much different backgrounds than mine. I never once received any special consideration from my keepers due to my profession or social status. However, my age, experience and legal knowledge gave me many opportunities to counsel and give legal help to fellow inmates of all ages and races, and I think that I always had the respect of the population and the staff (except for the two guys who punched me out, and I even got mellow with one of them over time.) That respect did make my time easier. Respect is the coin of the realm in prison.

I lifted heavy things, folded tens of thousands of T-shirts in a prison laundry, drove a truck in blizzards, herded cows, and worked through many nights. Not things that I was trained for in college or law school, but I'm here to tell about it.

PART I
The Fall

"If you want to know, I was
a lawyer before coming here.
Now, I am a judge-penitent."

Jean-Baptiste Clamance in
"The Fall"

Albert Camus

1

THE CHAIN

A ghostly white bus sat chugging diesel fumes that blended with the fog curling under the closed door in the garage of the King County Jail building. The air was early morning wet and concrete cold.

A thick, heavy door opened in a wall 100 feet from the bus, and a uniformed man stepped into the garage carrying a short, fat shotgun. At a barked command from the other side of the door, a line of 24 men, two abreast, snaked through the opening and shuffled toward the bus. They were dressed in thin, weathered orange jump suits and wore torn plastic shower slippers with no socks. Although it wasn't apparent, they wore no underwear underneath the "pumpkin suits".

A "ching-ching" sound came from the dragging of the slack in the chains that joined the inside ankles of each pair of men. The men were also connected by short chains attached to other chains strung around each of their waists. Still more chains tethered steel handcuffs in an 8-inch length from the waist chains. The handcuffs were bound together by six-inch chains.

I was the man on the left, third pair from the front, shackled to the tall black man with a high, sculpted pompadour, a man whom I would come to know as "George the Pimp".

As we started forward through the door from the inner building, my partner asked if I had done this before. I said, "No, this is my first time", and felt instantly stupid at the trite singles-bar line. It obviously was not his first time, and he briskly instructed me to move in step with him. As our technique improved with each step, I had the feeling that I had done this before. But, where? This was my second day of imprisonment, and I had never been chained up before. Then I remembered winning the three-legged race at a picnic when I was 12 years old, which demanded a similar technique. Amazing the stuff that lodges in our brain cells, to be recalled when needed.

We got up the steps and into the bus with surprising efficiency. Since we were only the third pair to get in, there were many empty seats, standard two-person bus seats. My experienced mentor took charge. He moved into one seat and directed me into the seat in front of it. That didn't make sense to me at first, but I soon saw the light. We backed into our respective seats, toward the side of the bus, with the chain which connected us at the waist running over the top of the seat back between us, and extended our legs toward the aisle as we went. When our backs were against the side of the bus, we sat down, directing the waist chain down in the space between the intervening seat back and the wall. Our ankle chain stretched across the side of that seat in the aisle. We were then able to sit relatively comfortably with our backs against the side of the bus and stretch our legs out the entire length of our seats. Without this trick we would have had to sit side by side in one seat, with very little leg room. We had a three-hour trip ahead of us, so every little advantage was important. Some of the cross-state trips to transport inmates are as much as ten hours long!

This was my first "con-wise" trick. I would learn many more in the years to come.

We sat for a long time with nothing happening Maybe a half hour. Only a guess, because my watch had been taken from me along with my other belongings when I checked in the King County Jail the day before to begin my 5-year imprisonment. Finally, two uniformed Department of Corrections officers climbed into the bus. One moved into the driver's seat, and the other, the one carrying the shot gun, closed and locked the steel screen gate between us and them and took a jump seat facing us, riding "shot gun" in the most literal sense of the term.

The bus started forward with a diesel rumble and lumbered out through the garage door, turning left up the steep hill to the southbound onramp to Interstate 5. The Interstate runs directly behind the King County Jail, which is an eleven-story building in downtown Seattle. At almost any hour in any day you can see women, sometimes with children, standing uphill from the freeway, waving at the upper floors of the jail building, where they know their men are watching through the narrow slit windows. Love will survive!

The bus merged into the early morning I-5 traffic and picked up speed in the fast lane as it headed south. It was a mysterious ghost ship, gliding through the fog, with no identifying markings to indicate that it had a cargo of criminals, some dangerous and some not, but all rendered harmless for the time being by chains, guards and a shotgun. The windows were only narrow slits in the sides of the bus, high enough up so that no one could see the passengers from the outside.

I was a passenger on "The Chain". That is the literally appropriate name for any transportation of convicts between any of the prison facilities in the State of

Washington. Every state has a similar procedure, with a similar name. No matter how low the security level of the prisoners at either end of the trip may be—murderers or unthreatening forgers or white collar thieves like me—convicts in transit are handled as dangerous killers.

On the traveling day, the prisoners are awakened as early as 4:00 a.m. and taken to a debarkation room where they are striped naked. They are given orange jumpsuits with "D.O.C." stenciled across the back and cheap slippers, usually some sort of shower shoes. No socks. No underwear. If you escape, you are not going to be well shod for running, or dressed for mixing in with the population.

A guard conducts a strip search for contraband before the prisoner puts on his traveling suit. The routine is always the same:

"Face me!"

"Raise your arm"

"Show me the palms and backs of your hands!"

"Open your mouth!"

"Raise your tongue!"

"Lift your scrotum!"

"Turn around!"

"Bend over!"

"Spread your cheeks!"

"Show me the bottoms of your feet!"

"Put on your clothes!"

The first time, the cheek spreading exercise is humiliating. But I realized after many strip searches, on the many occasions in which they were deemed necessary, that mooning a guard is one of the rare opportunities to show contempt without risk of punishment. I used to tell the officers, "I'd rather show it to you than look at it!"

Prison staff seem to be obsessed with the idea that inmates walking around with contraband up their asses, which would certainly require some serious sphincter control. Not that it is not done sometimes. But, the guards can never bring themselves to look sufficiently close to get a good look. The ritual is probably intended more as a humbling, "We own your ass!" gesture than as a serious investigative exercise. Pat downs are much more common, and an inmate is subjected to these many times a day. Over the years, to sneak food back to my "house" or to move something else from one place to another, I became so good that I bragged I could get a watermelon through a pat down, without putting it up my ass! Another con-wise achievement. Incidentally, to sneak something past a search by putting it up your ass is to "keister" it, which makes sense.

The "Chain", with me as a passenger, headed south toward the Washington Corrections Center at Shelton, 95 miles southwest of Seattle. I could see out of the slit window above me by raising myself with my elbows on the seat backs. I saw buildings, airports and forests go by that I had passed thousands of times, but never while chained to a heroin salesman and pimp, headed for 5 years in prison.

2

A SMALL TASTE OF IMPRISONMENT

On a Tuesday morning six months earlier, I sat in the courtroom of the Presiding Criminal Judge in the King County Superior Court, on the top floor of the King County Courthouse in downtown Seattle, directly across the street from the jail. A sky bridge on that floor joins the two buildings. I had been in the courtroom a great many times in my thirty years as a lawyer, and on this day I was dressed in my lawyer clothes—a conservative gray suit, button-down blue dress shirt, striped tie and black tasseled loafers. My dress was under the force of a habit that I had not yet shed.

For security, due to the exclusively criminal nature of the court's clientele, the sitting area was separated from the judge's bench and the courtroom furniture by a thick, soundproof window. Sound issued from within only when someone was called inside over the intercom. I sat among the collection of Usual Suspects, mostly young black men, and their posses. They obviously thought that I was a lawyer, and not one of them. Actually, I was both. I was waiting to be arraigned on 3 counts of Securities Fraud and 13 counts of Theft in the First Degree, resulting from my having lured some people into questionable investments and converting half a million dollars of my legal clients' monies.

The Presiding Criminal Judge was Janice Niemi, a good friend and law school classmate of mine. I had, in fact, been her campaign manager in her first two judicial election campaigns, first for the District Court, then for the Superior Court.

The scene inside the window was the usual criminal calendar madhouse, with more than fifty defendants being rushed to various stages of justice. My attorney was to the side, talking to the deputy prosecutor. I saw him look over his shoulder at Judge Niemi, who obviously had said something to him, although I couldn't hear her through the glass. He walked over to the side of the judge's bench and the two of them held a whispered conversation in front of the milling crooks and counsel. He looked up at me as they talked, then nodded to the judge and walked to the door in the windowed wall. The bailiff let him through and he came over to where I was sitting. He leaned over:

"Judge Niemi asked me to find out if you are comfortable with her handling this".

"Sure", I said. "Ask her if I can enter a plea and be sentenced now. She owes me!"

No such luck, but, a nice try anyway. I told my lawyer that it was ok with me for Judge Niemi to handle the arraignment, and he went back into the courtroom. After about fifteen more minutes my name was squawked over the sound system, and I got up and walked to the door. The bailiff let me in, and my lawyer motioned for me to stand beside him in front of the judge. I had, of course done this hundreds of times, but I had always stood on the right, where the lawyers stand, not on the left, the place for the crooks.

There was the usual bustle and confusion of files being located and passed, and whispers between counsel and court clerks. Judge Niemi looked at me with a grim smile and said,

"Hello, Nelson ."

"Hello, Your Honor. Nice to see you", I replied.

It was a private, bittersweet moment in the frantic courtroom. Nice to be treated with friendly respect, but painful to be there in the circumstances. A final "Aloha" to me as a lawyer. At that instant I ceased to have any illusions as to being a professional in my accustomed environment. A professional crook, yes. A professional lawyer, no.

We went through the standard moves. The deputy prosecutor from the Fraud Division who was assigned to my case read off the three counts of Securities Fraud and thirteen counts of Theft in the First Degree with which I was charged. The Securities Fraud charges were for loans totaling about $150,000 that I had arranged for myself, in which I had not recorded the deeds of trust on real property that I had promised to the lenders. The theft charges were for my having taken a total of about $250,000 from my trust account, in varying amounts, from the funds of thirteen of my clients.

I pled "Not Guilty" to all of the charges, which a defendant nearly always does at the arraignment stage of a criminal case. Not that I had any doubt about my guilt, or had any intent of fighting the general nature of the charges. However, I had not yet finished negotiations with the Prosecution Attorney for a plea bargain. That would continue in the coming weeks. In the normal course of events, the defendant eventually agrees to plead guilty to fewer than all of the initial charges, which the prosecutor has loaded up as his maximum wad in order to get the hammer in negotiations. When a defendant is faced with sixteen counts, which could conceivably lead to a ten year sentence, it is easier to get him to plead guilty to nine counts, which can give him five years. Plea bargaining is often criticized as a "soft on crime" process. In reality, the prosecution holds all the cards and uses the process to bludgeon out guilty pleas. With unpredictable, criminal-fearing juries, and judges who have to face election every four years and do not want to appear to the electorate to be too lenient, a defendant facing a possible very long sentence is usually scared as hell of going to trial. In my case, I wasn't anxious to face a jury. I knew that I had committed all of the crimes charged against me, although I could have quibbled over some of the technicalities, as my own conditioned lawyer's mind was sometimes tempted to do. I also knew that the sentencing judge would have broad discretion under the law relating to crooked lawyers, and could stick me with as many as ten years in prison, and most likely would do so if the prosecution recommended such a sentence.

I had in fact been negotiating with the prosecutor for over a year, while I liquidated properties and took other steps to pay back the money that my clients had lost. I was successful in paying back nearly $400,000, and that was a significant advantage in my plea bargaining. Still, in spite of my good efforts, the prosecutor recommended a 5 year sentence. I had hoped for something closer to 3 years. I didn't see why I should do more time than a child molester. They usually get about 3 ½ years for a first offense. However, the powers that be in society, the "grownups" as I think of them, have a bigger thing about crooked lawyers than they do about child molesters. One crime only affects children, while the other involves money. You can see the difference. There is also a very pronounced tendency for the legal community to want to visibly discipline its own miscreants, for public relations purposes. The result is sort of like dogs jumping on one of their injured brothers. Not a pretty picture.

It may seem strange, but I was quite relieved to finally know that my outside exposure was 5 years. I guess you had to be there. On a 5 year sentence, with one third off for "good time", I would serve 40 months in prison. Not like a week at the spa, but 8-to-10 years, which I most likely would have gotten after a jury conviction, is, as we say in prison, a Long Fucking Time!

There was also an intangible factor of personal redemption. While I was doing my time in the succeeding years, I read newspaper accounts of other lawyers who were caught up in circumstances similar to my own. In each case, they fought the Bar Association's investigation, rather than throwing up their hands and fully cooperating as I had. This served them well, as the prosecutor generally lets the Bar Association put his case together for him, and the Bar has limited assets and personnel. If you can outspend them, as Michael Milikin did with the Feds, you can get a good result. Then, when the cases came before the court, the accused lawyers whined the typical white collar lament that they had "suffered enough" from their disbarment and their fall in societal standing, and the sentencing judges surprisingly seemed to go along with it. An upper class mindset, I guess.

In the cases I read about, crooked lawyers got sentences of 18 to 24 months for the same thing that I got 60 months for. But the element that I identified in each case was that in order to take the posture that they did before the Bar and the court these people had to convince themselves that they themselves were somehow innocent and were being wronged by the process. Not to be sanctimonious about it, but I wanted to come clean and face the music for what I had done. Not to the extent of eating up the rest of my life with a 10 year sentence, but to at least accept what the law regarded as just deserts for my actions, all things considered. I sought to ameliorate my situation by making financial amends, rather than by minimizing my crimes. In the long run, I came out satisfied that things had balanced out.

At the end of my arraignment, I got another reminder that my status in the courtroom had changed radically. After Judge Niemi was through with me, my lawyer motioned me over to the side of the courtroom and we sat down. He pointed out a heavy-set man in a cheap suit and thin necktie who was sitting at a table along one wall, with a canvas bag at his feet.

"I have an appointment," my lawyer said. "Just follow that guy when he goes."

My lawyer seemed a little uneasy when he said that. He didn't offer any explanation, and I got the feeling that I was in for something that he didn't want to talk about. Funny, but over the months that we went through the process, I learned that my lawyer was typical of criminal attorneys, in that while he was comfortable in the courtroom setting of a criminal case, he knew almost nothing about what happens to his clients after they go through the door into the penal system, and he wasn't comfortable talking about the little that he did know. Even in my unusual case, in which I fully acknowledged my guilt and was reconciled to going to prison, he seemed reluctant to make me face the fact that I was going to be a *prisoner* behind *bars*! He maintained a sort of, "Don't worry. Everything is going to be ok", air. But, of course, everything *wasn't* really going to be ok!

I sat there continuing to look like a lawyer for another half hour. Then Beefy Boy got up and headed for the door through which I had seen defendants in red jail coveralls come and go at various intervals in the afternoon. He glanced over his shoulder at me and gestured slightly toward the door with his head. I got up and followed him. He held the door open and I walked through into a long hallway painted in an institutional yellow-brown that lacked the decorational dignity of the courtroom. In the wall to my right was a thick, scratched Plexiglas window looking into a small holding cell which was packed with a half dozen black women in faded and worn red coveralls. One of them had her face pressed against the wall and was insanely screaming words that I couldn't hear. The thought crept over me that I was now a part of her world.

The gentleman followed me into the hallway, and the door closed behind him.

"Please face the wall on your left, Sir, spread your feet, and place your hands on the wall above your head", he commanded with formal cop politeness.

"Oh shit!", I thought. "Am I going into that cell with those women?"

The cop patted me down and ran his hands up the inside of my legs, looking for concealed weapons or contraband. This was the first of hundreds, if not thousands, of "pat downs" that I would experience in the coming years.

"Hands behind your back, Sir."

I complied again, and he "cuffed me up". The handcuffs bit into my wrists, but I figured that this was as much due to my inexperience in things of this matter as to brutality on his part.

I walked across the sky bridge to the jail building in my suit, tasseled loafers and handcuffs, with the officer a few regulation steps behind me. When we reached the other side, he directed me into an elevator and we went down several floors. We got out, and he marched me into a long room that had a counter with a number of uniformed deputies behind it on the left, and a big holding cell across from the counter. There was a large Plexiglas window looking into the cell. I stood in front of the counter and a deputy asked me for all my personal property. I gave him my pen, watch, belt, wallet and car keys. He listed them on an inventory sheet and put them in a brown paper bag. I signed the inventory, and it and the sack disappeared behind the counter.

The lock on the holding cell made a loud "WHAP!" noise, and the door slid open sideways, apparently operated from a remote switch behind the counter. I was directed into the cell, where I found myself with a dozen other gentlemen. They were all dressed in street clothes, not jail coveralls. I was the best dressed by far. Although the business area occupied by the deputies was clean and orderly like a normal office setting, the holding cell, only a few feet away, had a transient jail squalor that cannot be scrubbed away. Stains of scores of unidentified substances covered the walls. The smell of sweat, urine and tobacco hung in a thick mixture in the air. Smoking was theoretically not permitted, but two of my cell mates were sitting together on the wet floor next to a toilet which was set behind a 3-foot-high concrete privacy barrier at one end of the room, sharing a cigarette. In my years in prison, I would witness the passion and initiative that people had for tobacco in places where it was prohibited. I marveled at the amount of daily effort that went into smoking, and recognized how much my own burden was lessened by not having the habit.

To my surprise, there were two telephones on the wall which you could use to make free personal calls, to take care of the proverbial "one phone call", I suppose. I could have ordered a pizza, but delivery would probably have been difficult. As it happened, there were a couple of young dudes camping on the two phones, talking to their homies or girlfriends, so I was unable to use the phones. Not that I had anyone I wanted to call from there.

My name was called on the intercom after about 45 minutes, and the latch on the door slapped open. I went out and was taken through the booking process. In spite of the tremendous advances that have taken place in the interpretation of fingerprints, the fingerprinting process itself has not changed since the whole rigmarole began. Slow, repetitive and sloppy. The officer who took my prints had bad body odor, but I was not in a position to complain.

The mug shot technology *has* advanced. A digital camera produced a very distinguished photograph of me in suit and tie, with a number across my chest, like in the movies. All of my data was automatically printed on the page with the picture.

When the fingerprinting and the photographing were completed, I was led back to the counter in the long room. The deputy handed me my property sack and called, "One out!" He looked up at me and said, "You can go." In five minutes I was on the street and my introduction to imprisonment was over.

I called my son that night and told him about my hour in prison. He asked, "Did you get a tattoo?"

3

THROUGH THE LOOKING GLASS

When I had gotten as far as I could with plea negotiations, we set a "change of plea" hearing, at which I would plead guilty to a reduced charge of two counts of Securities Fraud and eight counts of Theft, with the prosecutor recommending a sentence of 5 years. The prosecutor agreed to set the hearing for a month away, to put it after the wedding of the daughter of Mavis, my partner of many years. I didn't want to be splashed all over the newspapers like a mafia don before the wedding, particularly since I would be singing at the Catholic ceremony. I wonder if there is some sort of Guinness Book of Records category for a person who sings The Lord's Prayer to 250 people on a Saturday and pleads guilty to 10 felony counts on the following Monday. If there is, look for me in the next edition!

I was sentenced on October 22, 1998, to 60 months in the Department of Corrections, which meant that I would go to one or the other of approximately 10 prison facilities in Washington State. One-third off for good behavior and programming meant that I would serve 40 months. That's three years and four months, if you do the math. I felt that I would have no problem achieving the requisite standard of "good behavior" in a population of criminals. However, I was to discover that it isn't that simple. You get 1/6 off for good behavior, which means having no major infractions, and 1/6 off for "programming", which means completing a bunch of pain-in-the ass classes which are not designed for a person with seven years of college. I later had to ask myself why a guy who spends his clients' money needs to take an anger management class. I wasn't angry! The answer, in bureaucratic logic, is that there have to be enough people taking the class to keep it going, or else some state employee loses his job.

I rounded the sentence off in my mind to three years. Somewhat more than I had wanted, but not too bad, considering that I had stolen a half million dollars. Three years earlier, when Mavis and I were sitting on a cliff over looking the

South Pacific on the Coromandel Peninsula in New Zealand, planning our life out, I said, "I can handle a couple of years in prison."

The sentencing judge gave me ten days to get my act together. I was to turn myself in at the King County Jail by noon on Monday, November 2. I had made a deal with the prosecutor to stay out until after Thanksgiving, but the judge wouldn't go along with it. She said, "I usually just send them across the street right away." I was lucky to get ten days.

In Washington State, all entrants into the prison system start at the county jail level in the county where they are sentenced. You can't avoid that step by just showing up at a prison in a limo, which would be nice.

King County Jail is a very unpleasant place. The Chain from there to the admissions center at the Washington Corrections Center in Shelton runs on Tuesdays, so it is best to check into King County Jail on Monday, if you have a choice, so you can transfer on Tuesday morning, avoiding a long stay in "county".

I had spent a few pleasant months in anticipation of going into prison for three years-plus. In July, Mavis and I visited my youngest daughter, Erica, in New York City for a week, and we did the town, from Harlem to Battery Park. Her daughter's wedding and several days of related festivities were in August. Then, she set up a great road trip for us down the Oregon and Northern California coasts to Napa Valley, where we did the wineries and had an unforgettable 18 course dinner—that's right...18 courses!—at the French Laundry in Yountsville, rated by many as the best restaurant in the U.S. Then, in September we flew to San Francisco for a friend's wedding and some sentimental time at a few places special to us. Finally, as a valedictory in the week before I was to leave the Free World, Mavis stood me to dinner at several of my favorite Seattle restaurants. The kid knows how to treat a soon-to-be convict. God knows, it was the last really good food that I was to taste for a long time!

On the morning of November 2, 1998, I fussed around putting some things away in the house, but there really wasn't anything that needed doing. At 10.00 a.m. we got in the car and headed downtown to the jail. Once on our way, we realized that we had lots of time before the noon deadline. I didn't want to check in early, and it didn't make sense to burn time driving around the block, so we stopped for coffee at a Starbucks on Capital Hill, close to downtown. I had a double cappuccino. If I had foreseen the barren coffee world that lay before me, I would have savored the drink more appreciatively. I later came to realize that I certainly had not listened closely enough to the judge when she pronounced my sentence. I am now sure that what she said was:

"I sentence you to five years of bad coffee. May God have mercy on your soul!"

That's cruel and unusual punishment for a guy from Seattle!

We finished up at Starbucks at 11:30 and drove down the hill to the King County Jail building. We had said our goodbyes, so we didn't do any unseemly smooching in the car. A peck on the cheek, and I was out the car door and on my way down the street to the jail building entrance. I looked back once, but she was gone. She had a different life ahead of her for a few years too. "One less bell to answer...."

I had tried to find out what personal effects I could take with me when I checked into the System for 5 years. At my age, I couldn't imagine that I wasn't responsible for taking care of the small personal items of life like a toothbrush, a razor, shampoo, comb, underwear...the bare minimum essentials. No one had done that for me in my life, even in the Navy. My attorney couldn't tell me, consistent with his knowledge void about nearly everything that happens after a guilty verdict. My telephone calls to the King County Jail and the Washington Corrections Center ended up in dead-end recording networks of useless connections relevant to nothing. Finally, after an hour of, "For........., press.......", I got through to an inmate working in the kitchen at the Washington Corrections Center.

"Hello", I said. "I'm checking into your place next week and I'm wondering what I'm supposed to bring."

"Nothing!"

"Not even a toothbrush?"

"They give you that."

"Underwear?"

"No!"

Well, it's said that we come into this world naked and leave it naked. Add to that that we go to prison naked!

I had dressed lightly for my surrender at the King County Jail, with as few possessions as I could wear and carry without being arrested for indecent exposure and vagrancy. I wore jeans without a belt, a flannel shirt with no undershirt, socks, running shoes and underwear. No jacket, even though it was a brisk November day, since I thought I would only have to walk a half block to the entrance to the jail building. I wore eye glasses, not knowing if I would be permitted to have contact lenses. (It would be many months before I managed to work that detail through the bureaucratic maze) I had my driver's license in my pocket in case I had to prove who I was in order to get in.

I walked in the front door of the jail building, which I had done many times when representing criminal defendants other than myself. I approached the deputy sheriff who sat at the duty desk guarding the entrance.

"I'm checking into jail. Where do I go?"

Apparently no one had ever come in that door for that purpose. The guard's reply was, "Huh?"

"How do I get in here? I'm going to prison, and I was told that this is where I have to start."

"Well," he said, "I'm not sure. Most prisoners don't just walk in here under their own power. The arresting officer usually drives them into the garage in the side of the building, and they take them in from there. No one has ever come in the front door while I've been here. I think you should go around there. There's a door that says 'Admitting', with a button beside it. Push the button and a voice will come on."

I walked back out to the sidewalk I thought, "Well, I tried and they wouldn't take me. Maybe I can go home." I had heard that if a man survives a hanging they have to cut him down and let him go. Was I free to go? Somehow, I didn't think it would work.

I walked to the corner and up the hill where Mavis had disappeared. Halfway up, I turned into the garage and saw the "Admitting" door that the guard had told me about. I pushed the button by the door. I couldn't hear a buzz or any other indication that the button was connected to anything. I pushed it again. A distorted metallic voice said,

"What?"

"I'm trying to get into jail."

"You're what?"

"Is this where I go to jail?"

"Who are you?"

"I'm a person who is supposed to report to jail here before noon, and it's ten to twelve now."

"Isn't there an officer with you?"

"No."

"Just a minute."

Nothing happened for about five minutes. Then the metal voice rasped,

"You can't come in this door without an officer. Go around to the door in the alleyway in the middle of the building."

I walked back out onto the sidewalk. There was a narrow walkway downhill about five yards from the garage door. I walked into it. At the end there was another door, with no sign indicating what it was or where it went, but there was a dirty window in the door. There was a button in the wall beside the door. I pushed it. I was getting finger fatigue!

I could see the dim outline of a uniformed officer through the window. He looked up at me, so I knew that he was aware that I was there. He looked way, and nothing happened for another twenty minutes. Finally he got up and walked over to the window. He pushed a button, and his voice came through a speaker that I couldn't see.

"What's your name?"

I told him my name.

"Just a minute."

He went back to his table and shuffled through some manila folders. He brought one to the window.

"Do you have any identification?"

You need references to get into jail? "Maybe with my credit rating they won't let me in!", I thought. "I hope it's not as hard to get out of prison as it is to get in!"

The guard let me through the door and I began the long booking process that reacquainted me with the indignities of the Strip and Body Cavity Search. I would get used to it in a very short time, as it seemed to happen almost every time I went from one room to another. All of my clothing and everything else I had with me, except my glasses, were taken from me and put in a hanger bag that appeared to have been designed for the purpose. Mavis received them in the mail a couple of weeks later. I ended up in a threadbare red jumpsuit over Fruit of the Loom briefs that obviously had had long service, but appeared to have been adequately laundered. It would be several months before I would see a pair of new underwear, shipped in from the outside. I was given relatively new Hawaiian style flip-flops for my feet.

After an accompanied trip through a warren of hallways and elevators, I found myself back in the holding cell that I had occupied when I was arraigned and booked several months earlier. Amazingly, I was put through the entire regime of photography and finger printing all over again, as if I had never been there before, leaving me with the impression that the process is as important for public employment as for criminal justice. I would learn over time that a great deal of prison procedure is in fact primarily concerned with public employment. The prisoners are a necessary inconvenience in the arrangement. My new picture did not have me in the nice suit that I wore in the earlier one.

I say "prisoners". In fact, however, throughout my prison experience, we were always referred to as "inmates", which I had thought was what you called people in a funny farm. I thought we were "convicts", but that term is used, if at all, for inmates inside the walls at maximum security facilities. Sometimes on printed forms, usually something that our friends or families had to fill out when they visited us, we were called "The Offender". That has a certain Swartznegger sound to it.

The holding cell was packed with my fellow members of the Criminal Element. This time I was not overdressed. My red jump suit looked just like everyone else's. The smell of sweat, urine and stale tobacco was still there.

I was, surprisingly, permitted a brief return visit to the polite world. When I had checked in, the officer asked some boiler-plate health questions. Basically, "Got any problems today?" I had disclosed to him a bandaged chemical burn on the top of my left foot, which I had suffered from spilling a virulent solvent while cleaning some greasy restaurant equipment in the auction business where I was working. The burn had partially healed and scabbed over, and then reached the stage where the scabs started breaking up, and the sore stuck to my sock. Yuck! So, I had put some gauze and tape over it. It was obvious that the guard thought that my story was a little fishy. In the environment of his day-to-day experience, my injury was more likely to have come from a chemical spill in a methamphetamine lab.

Anyway, when I had been in the holding cell for about an hour, I was called out to see the nurse, and I was directed down the hallway to a doorway with a "Clinic" sign above it. This was a brief return to the world of cleanliness and dignity. I would find on many occasions in the future months, in different institutions, that hospitals or clinics are islands of decency in the prison environment.

The nurse, a guy, changed the dressing on my foot and made a notation in my records. That notation would get me daily clinic visits for a dressing change for the next couple of weeks at my new prison home, a great break!

An hour or so after my visit to the clinic, four of us were called by name from the holding cell, and we took an elevator up to what must have been near the top of the building. We were directed to a pile of thin plastic-covered mattresses, grievously cracked and worn, and a wooden bin containing bedding rolls, which consisted of two condom-thin sheets and a towel, wrapped in a sad cotton blanket. There were also a toothbrush and a miniature tube of toothpaste, and a tiny bar of soap, like you get in a cheap motel. A deputy ordered us to roll out the bundles, and the authorities inspected the display for contraband, apparently forgetting that *they*, not we, had packed up the rolls. We then rolled them back up, and, with the mattress over one shoulder and the bedroll under the other arm, we shuffled through a heavy, grilled doorway into a room that immediately reminded me of the bridge of the Starship Enterprise. It was dark, with a raised control center in the middle. Panels of illuminated dials and red and green indicator lights showed eerily on the figures of the uniformed guards.

In a ring around the guard center were six dormitory cells. A large window showed the brightly lighted interior of each room. I was directed into one of them, my first prison home. I looked around the room, which was about 50 feet square. The walls were covered unevenly with many coats of shiny yellow/brown institutional paint. Fifteen built-in bed frames were variously located through the room. Pairs of upper and lower bunks were built into the walls, somewhat resembling cheap prefab plastic shower stalls from Sears, laid on their sides. A half dozen floor-level single bunks protruded perpendicularly from the back wall. The bunks were unnumbered, apparently regarded as fungibles by the management. No assigned seating or lying. I had my choice of available openings, which was one, an upper in the middle of the back wall. It was high enough that I couldn't climb into it except by stepping on the bunk below.

On neither that occasion nor any other have I experienced a prison upper bunk the entry to which had been considered by its designer. In cells that I occupied later in various institutions, I was able to avoid the annoying necessity of stepping on my cellie's bunk by climbing up via the toilet and/or washbowl.

Incidentally, the person with whom an inmate shares his living space, whether it is truly a cell or is a more comfortable room, is always referred to as his "cellie". There are unwritten rules of cooperation and support between cellies, although, like in all social relationships, the practice varies with the personalities. Over three and a half years, I had cellies who were Black, Mexican, Caucasian, Native American, Pakistani, Pilipino, Ukrainian and Korean. The only difficult combination was with a white man who had been a friend of sorts, and it was as much my fault as his. The basic problem involved television. I am from a family that did not always have a TV on in the background. My incompatible cellie was a compulsive viewer, and he favored World Federation of Wrestling events and NASCAR races, night and day. That can be a burden in an 8 by 10 room. He would leave the television on when he went to sleep at night, and if I turned it off at 2:00 a.m., he would wake up from the sudden silence and turn it back on. He would not wear headphones, which was a normal gesture of courtesy to cellies. We both blew our corks at the same time one weekend and almost got stuck in the doorway heading out to the duty desk to request a change of cellies. We got an amicable divorce, and we continued as friends.

Another of my cellies, a 21-year-old black man, always wore headphones when he watched television. He left the set on all night, which didn't bother me, because I could turn to the wall and close my eyes and shut out the light, a skill that I mastered early on. One night I was wakened by the distant sound of a woman's screams, which was particularly strange because we were in a forest work camp 30 miles from the nearest town. I looked up and saw that the movie "Jaws" was on the TV, and the giant white shark was making a meal of a screaming young lady. My cellie had the sound cranked up so high that I could hear the screams through the headphones that he wore. He slept peacefully through the carnage.

Television is a disease in prison, that does as much to impede personal development as it does on the streets. Fortunately, I was immune, and my time, so *much time*, would prove to be better spent.

However, in this first prison night in the King County Jail, a small black and white TV mounted high up on a wall carried Monday Night Football. It seemed like a priceless luxury.

4

DAY ONE OF TWELVE HUNDRED

My entry into the King County jail cell began a day of first-time experiences, as was the case with every day in the coming weeks. Making an upper bunk requires a technique that must resemble that of a Hindu fakir climbing one of those ropes that isn't tied to anything. The difficulty is enhanced by several factors unique to the prison environment. First, you have to size up the occupant of the lower bunk to decide whether you should risk standing on his bunk to reach the upper. On your first day in a mixed population prison containing a montage of criminal personalities, each bearing his incarceration in his own fashion, it is best to discard that option altogether. Later on, when you solve problems in the give and take of a more settled, long-term relationship with a cellie, standing on his bunk might be an acceptable part of a larger consensual tradeoff. When in doubt, you had best find yourself on the top bunk with your bedding, trying to levitate while you spread and tuck in the sheets and blankets that are under your knees. Add into the mix the factor that an inmate's bunk, being one of the only things that he has to himself, is a very personal possession. You *never*, in *any* circumstances, sit, let alone stand, on another inmate's bunk without his permission.

To me, properly making up one's bunk each morning in prison, especially in the close quarters of a high security two-man cell, is an important part of maintaining one's dignity and character. (More about two-man cells becoming *three-man* cells later!) Your bunk is the only piece of furniture that is exclusively yours. There is nothing else to sit, lie, read or write on, except perhaps the toilet, and that is just not done, for a number of reasons. Your bunk is more than a piece of furniture; it is your home for twenty hours a day. Even in a dormitory, it is the only place where you can find any measure of privacy, or what must pass for privacy in prison.

Aside from utility, the state of an inmate's bunk is an indicator of many characteristics, including self esteem and general adjustment. Good convicts, in their own estimation and in the estimation of others, have good bunks. Bad prisoners have bad bunks. It's really as simple as that, a nearly flawless stereotype for evaluating a prison population.

An obvious exception must be made for teen-age inmates, who are, to a man, generally incapable of making a bed. Or of getting *out* of it, for that matter. I spent a month in a cubicle with two 19-year-olds. My *in loco parentis* influence as a much older man brought them some way toward a minimally acceptable human level of orderliness by the end of our time together, but when I returned to retrieve a book after moving on to another tier, I found that they, along with my 20-something replacement, had regressed to a state of bed-ridden squalor.

I observed that sleep was the greatest cause of disciplinary problems in prison. Repeated small penalties for failing to get out of bed when required accumulate and eventually result in serious sanctions, such as "extra duty". Extra duty usually consists of 10-40 hours of menial cleaning tasks, in addition to whatever regular work duties the inmate has. Not performing the extra duty in a timely and satisfactory fashion, perhaps by again failing to get out of bed, brings down very serious consequences. Eventually, a guy can get on the slippery slope of a bad relationship with the cops, which was what we called the guards, and he is always in trouble. He gets thrown in the Hole, and may get transferred out to a harsher institution.

The phenomenon of an inmate "Sleeping away his time" is another story. Some men are able to sleep away a sentence of many years. When they get thrown into the Hole or are transferred to another institution, they just go back to bed!

On making up an upper bunk:

On your knees on the bunk, face the wall. Place all bedding, except the sheet that you are going to use for the bottom, in a pile toward the end of the bed, preferably against the wall so that nothing will get knocked off onto the floor. If one of the sheets is a fitted contour sheet or either of them is not thin enough to see through, you are not in prison, and you will eventually wake up from your bad dream.

Spread the bottom sheet over the length of the bed, with equal amounts extending past the ends of the mattress, in the ideal situation in which the sheet has not been shrunk to less than the size of the bed. If you are in prison, it will be too short, Do the best that you can. I found it best to favor the end where your head would be. I would rather have my feet than my face on the hard, cracked plastic mattress surface.

Let about one foot of the sheet hang over the outer edge of the bed away from the wall. This will require some shifting on your knees, and you may have to turn halfway around in each sideways direction to roughly measure the hanging distance. When you are satisfied that it is even, turn back to face the wall. Lift up the middle of the mattress against the wall with your left hand if you are right handed, the right if you are left handed, and with the free hand and arm scoop the center portion of the sheet under the mattress, pushing it as far in as possible and drawing it taut against the rest of the sheet, which is anchored by your knees. Then move to the right and left, in turn, and tuck in the remainder of the back edge of the sheet in the same fashion.

At this point, you have to climb back to the floor. As this cycle must be repeated for each sheet and blanket, it is a good idea, if possible, to undertake the whole operation while the occupant of the lower bunk is out of the cell for sick call or some other reason, if you have to step on his bunk to get in and out of your own. Again, however, every option other than stepping on the lower bunk should be explored.

Stand on the floor, facing the bed. Grab the front edge of the sheet with hands about two feet apart and pull it taut against the pressure of the tucked-in rear edge. Shove the sheet in as far as possible under the mattress, moving right and left to get it all in. Adjust as necessary to get a nice smooth surface. Tuck in the ends as tight as possible with the length available.

Climb back into the bunk and repeat the process for the top sheet. Allow a little less length for the front edge, perhaps eight inches, because you will be pulling that portion out when you climb into the bed. You will, of course, have more sheet to tuck in at the bottom, because this sheet will not be tucked in at the top. It is good to get a nice solid anchor at the bottom so the top sheet doesn't pull out from the pressure of your feet.

Finally, the blankets. You are usually issued two blankets in prison. If they are decent wool military blankets, warmth will not be a problem, and you will be able to lay them both in a single layer, with plenty of width to tuck in. Incredibly, I have been issued cotton mesh blankets in a stormy forest work camp, necessitating folding them over to a double thickness. That results in a narrow width, with little or nothing to tuck in. Shrinkage from repeated laundering also decreases tuck-in length and width. If you ever get hold of a new blanket in prison, you will be able to see by comparison that the other, older one is closer to the size of a postage stamp than a blanket.

Working with what you have, do your best with the first blanket, installing it in the same fashion as the top sheet. The top blanket is the same, except that you want to have a front edge hangover of at least 8", so you can miter the bottom corner. If you can put on that blanket without doubling it over, you will have plenty of material. If you must double it, miter the corner and tuck in the front edge first, before the side against the wall.

Mitering a sheet or blanket corner is a skill, like whistling through your teeth or wiggling your ears, that will impress people throughout your life. It takes practice, but you have plenty of time for practice in prison. It impresses prison guards while you are there, and it impresses chicks after you get out.

The most important thing in mitering is to tuck in the bottom end first, right up to the corner being mitered, leaving the long side edge hanging free to the point of that corner. Get a good, smooth tuck, without any bunching. Then grasp the bottom of the front edge with the hand farthest from the corner, about a foot toward the head of the bed. Lift it up, and a fold will extend diagonally down from your hand to a point at or near the top of the mattress corner. Adjust your grip as necessary to position the bottom end of the slant exactly on the corner. A portion of the material will then be hanging straight down from the inclined fold. With your other hand, tuck that portion tightly under the mattress. Holding the untucked remainder against the top edge of the mattress, bring the raised hand down with its handful and you should have a nicely mitered corner. Tuck in the remainder of the material along the front edge of the mattress. Drop a quarter from a height of 18" above the mattress to test your skill. Just kidding! You don't have any coins in prison.

Of course it won't work the first time. The Ginza knife doesn't work the day you get it in the mail from Ted Turner. Practice makes perfect.

I dumped my ragged plastic mattress on my King County Jail upper bunk and made the bed up in a sloppy fashion. I had not yet developed the skills and techniques that I described above, and the materials that I was working with were of particularly poor quality, even by prison standards. You just can't get a good, holding tuck with a gossamer thin sheet on a slick plastic mattress. Anyway, I only planned to be there one night.

This was my first taste of prison, and my first insertion into prison society. The fifteen of us were all transients of one nature or another, on our way to more permanent residences. On other floors of the jail building, men lived in similar conditions for many months, waiting for their trials. "County", as time in a county jail is referred to, is the worst time you can do, even worse than the tightest maximum security prison. The setting is squalid, the food is ghastly and there is no recreation or exercise whatsoever. It is not so bad, I am told, in smaller counties. The jail in San Juan County, in Friday Harbor in the San Juan Islands, is so small and lightly populated that no food service is maintained. The inmates order off a menu from the restaurant next door to the courthouse, which is a very good small town eatery. But King County Jail is hell.

There was a television set bolted to a wall, and, as I said earlier, we got to watch Monday Night Football. Not a high definition set by any means! The shower and toilet were in a separate room opening off one end of the dormitory, without a door. This would prove to be the last time for nearly three months that I could shower when I wanted to. I skipped an evening shower.

There were two toilets, of the indestructible stainless steel design that has a built-in seat molded into the body, so it can't be raised when you are peeing into it. The problem of a wet toilet seat had been solved by someone by the posting of handwritten signs on the wall above the toilets. One said "SHITTER" and the other said "PISSER". It appeared that an orderly behavior followed these instructions, with the inmates shitting on the SHITTER and pissing only in the PIS-SER. That was a comfort. I was learning that in prison small things can be important.

I had arrived in time for dinner. In fact, as in the best of restaurants, I had a reservation! But no choice of entrees, and no wine list.

Meals are served early in prison. I wasn't used to eating dinner at 4:30. However, once you get on prison time, it's all relative. You eat breakfast at 6:00 a.m., and then 11:00 a.m. doesn't seem too early for lunch. Then, your stomach starts to growl for dinner by 4:00.

At King County, the meals were wheeled to the cell door in covered trays on a tiered cart. We all had to line up at the door like barnyard animals before anyone could get his food. I was only there for two meals, but we had a problem both times with an Ethiopian man who never got out of his bunk. It took some very bad threats from a very bad looking resident of the room to get him up both times.

When we were all bunched at the door, an inmate porter accompanied by a guard uncovered the trays and handed them to us, one at a time. My stomach churned when I looked at my big burrito, covered with redeye gravy, with some mushy string beans on the side. Sixty months of this ahead of me! Even forty months, with time off for good behavior, means 3,600 meals, and it wasn't looking good for my guts. Fortunately, however, that dinner and the breakfast the next morning were the two worst meals, by far, that I saw in all my time in prison.

I ate some of the burrito. When in Rome.... I thought of that burrito months later when I was reading "Alive", the story about the Bolivian plane crash victims who survived by eating their companions, and wondered which I would have chosen, the burrito or the human drumstick.

Breakfast the next morning was a thick, sticky cornmeal mush, with Tang to drink. No milk or sugar. Some of the men poured their Tang over the mush. After each meal the trustee would come back to collect the trays. The utensils were thrown away, tiny white plastic pieces that looked like Barbie Doll tableware. It would take a month to eat a bowl of soup with the spoon. After the trays were recovered, a push broom, dustpan, mop bucket and mop were shoved into the room. If the room wasn't swept and mopped in 15 minutes, the next meal wouldn't happen. As in nearly all of my group work experiences in prison, the work was put away diligently and cheerfully by the inmates. Prisoners are always far better workers than the public employees who supervise them, and are constantly frustrated by the bureaucratic sloth that surrounds them.

I slept surprisingly well my first night in incarceration. I was, however, introduced to the cacophony of snoring that fills any room full of sleeping men. I showered before my cornmeal mush breakfast and reduced my wafer of soap to a sliver. I pissed in the PISSER.

While the floor was getting its post-breakfast mopping, the public address system squawked, "Rupert! Christensen! Johnson! Roll up your bunks and report to the door!" It was 6:00 a.m. I rolled my bedding and towel up in the mattress and carried the package to the door. The other two men who had been called did the same. In a few minutes the lock slammed and the door slid open. A guard motioned us out. We walked back over the route that I had taken coming in the day before and were directed to throw the mattresses on a pile and dump everything else in a wooden bin. I did as I was told and stood in the hallway with absolutely no worldly possessions other than my threadbare jumpsuit and my shower shoes.

Another 20 men from other cells joined us, all bound for transfer out of King County Jail. We were accompanied down an elevator by a guard in groups of 5 or 6. I was in an elevator with five men, all of whom were clearly younger than 25. At a stop, a fatherly looking black officer, older than me, got in the elevator. On the way down, he looked around at the group, then at me. He said to me, "I don't feel sorry for you. These young people aren't old enough to know better, but you are!"

Well, fuck you very much! I didn't say anything. I hadn't expected the special attention.

We were still dressed in our red jail jumpsuits and plastic shower shoes. We were herded into a small room, where we were told to select replacement footwear from a wooden bin. I rummaged through at least a hundred torn plastic slippers of the design that covers the first three or so inches of the front of the foot, different enough to distinguish left from right. There were no lefts! Had a troupe of dancers, all with the proverbial "two left feet", been jailed? Whatever the reason, I was hobbled for most of the remainder of the day by being shod in two right slippers. The one on my left angled inward from the front, so that my heel was only halfway in it.

We filed through a doorway into another holding cell, 25 men with benches for 15. There was a toilet of the ever-present stainless steel, fixed seat design, of which the men made continuous, immodest use.

Nothing happened for almost an hour. Nearly all of the men were black. From their conversations, it appeared that most of them had gone through this routine before. There were three young white kids, who couldn't have been more than 19 years old. They were all fairly slight of build, and all blond. Just what you don't want to be when you go to prison! They were visibly nervous, and scared shitless. A group of the older men were enjoying the kids' discomfort, and were enhancing it by remarks like, "Fresh meat!" Later in the day when we checked into the Washington Corrections Center at the end of our trip on the Chain, we were each asked, "Is there anyone who you feel threatened by? Do you feel that you need protection?" The three kids disappeared at that point and I didn't see anything of them for several weeks, when they turned up for an education level test, dressed in white coveralls. That uniform indicated that they had been "PC'd up", which means that they went into Protective Custody.

As we sat in the holding cell, we were still in our red King County Jail jumpsuits. We were about to undergo a clothing change and to get "chained up" for our trip. One at a time, we filed through a doorway into a small room where three officers in Department of Corrections uniforms were at work. The first step was to strip off our red jumpsuits and pick up an orange one from a one-size-fits-all pile on the floor. These were much too large for some men, and skin-tight for others. Not to worry. Appearance isn't a big deal on the Chain. After putting on my orange suit, with "D.O.C." stenciled across the back, I stood next to my randomly happenstance traveling partner, a tall black man with a high pompadour hairdo. One of the officers put chains around each of our waists and connected those two chains with another one, about a foot long. Another officer put chains around our inner ankles and connected those with another foot-long chain. Finally, the third officer put handcuffs on us and connected the cuffs to our waist chains with still another chain, less than a foot long. The final situation was that we two convicts were chained together at the waist and ankle, and our cuffed wrists were connected to our waists, with not quite enough freedom to pick a nose.

A white man and a black man tethered together like Tony Curtis and Sidney Portier in "The Defiant Ones", we shuffled through the doorway to the garage and lined up at the side of the Chain bus, where this story began.

5

WHERE'S THE WELCOME WAGON?

The white ghost bus angled off Interstate 5 at the State Capitol in Olympia and headed west toward the Pacific Ocean. After about 45 minutes, I could see a highway sign through the metal grill between the front windshield and me:

WASHINGTON STATE PATROL ACADEMY

WASHINGTON CORRECTIONS CENTER

We exited to the right and turned left under the freeway, heading north past the military style buildings of the State Patrol facility and through a large, open field. As he must enjoy reciting 200 times a year, the guard at the front of the bus announced,:

"This is the State Patrol target range. They practice on escaping prisoners!"

No laughter from the passengers.

Shortly, we were gliding alongside what looked like an aging community college campus. Neatly mowed lawns, with sculpted hedges and low 1950's-style buildings. A baseball diamond surrounded by a running track, guard towers, fences topped with razor wire…. Guard towers? Razor wire? I was not going "back to school"!

The bus turned in a heavily guarded gate through a high cyclone fence. I noticed electrical insulators carrying conductors that attached to the fence at intervals, obviously designed to fry escaping inmates. The bus stopped inside the gate and the guard left the bus with his shotgun and came back without it. Firearms are not carried within an institution, but they are available in an armory that can be broken open quickly in emergencies, like riots. Also, the guards in the towers at the corners of the property are armed with rifles and scopes.

The bus rolled across the grounds, turned a couple of corners, and stopped in front of the entrance to a plain one-story building. We clanked out of the seats and awkwardly made our way down and out of our transportation and serpentined our way into the building. We entered a long, low-ceilinged room with five steel-fenced areas on the right. Each enclosure had a locked gate, inside of which were wooden benches to seat about 80 men. Two of the compounds were filled with earlier arrivals, one group in the same orange traveling jumpsuits as ours, and the other comparatively smartly decked out in navy blue coveralls over white undershirts, with spiffy new black Converse low cuts, just like the "tennis shoes" that we used to wear for all sports in the 1950's, before the Footwear Revolution. Already conditioned to rejoice at small benefits, my spirits soared at the sight of this upscale prison garb. I felt a faith that where there are undershirts there are underpants. And the prospect of getting into new shoes...with socks!...was mind-boggling. It may have taken Patty Hearst months to break in captivity, but I was ready after less than 24 hours to kill, or betray my country and loved ones, for underwear and a pair of shoes!

As we stood in a line, still shackled in pairs, four guards worked down the row, taking off our chains. Let me tell you, there are very few events in life more gratifying than having full body chains and handcuffs taken off. It never lost its effect in all of the occasions that I experienced it.

This was my first contact with the order of people who, in one capacity or another, would govern every aspect of my life for several years. "Prison Guard" is a term that is chock full of visions, fears and emotions, pretty much all bad. My first impression of my new captors was that they were, overall, fairly jovial good old Mason County country boys, with lots of facial hair and enormous beer guts rolling over 50" trouser waists. As I later changed institutions, I changed rural counties, but the stereotype held. The State must issue beards and beer guts as a part of the uniform. And that's just the *female* guards!

The Washington Corrections Center is in Shelton, Washington, in Mason County; logging country, or what used to be logging country before the Spotted Owl decimated the industry. Throughout the Washington State prison system, the place is referred to as the "R-Units", for reasons which will become obvious. Most of the state's prison facilities are in similar rural areas of high unemployment, and serve as much as working welfare centers for grossly overweight, marginally literate country folks as safe storage for law breakers. From a prisoner's point of view, they are decent masters, easy to get along with and, to some extent, to manipulate, as long as you play pretty much by the general basic rule of good behavior, which means that you don't do anything to make their job harder.

Nepotism is thick in the rural prisons—husbands and wives, brothers and sisters, fathers and sons and daughters are often on the same payroll—so the staff draws from a consistent gene pool. Genial, uncomplicated country people, who are happy in a simple, comfortable employment, and who repay the inmates' good behavior with a basic decency. I was to learn over the months and years ahead of me that the punishment of prison confinement is not about being subjected to cruelty or even discomfort, even the annoying bureaucratic pettiness, but to be isolated from contact with loved ones and the freedoms of normal, everyday life.

Once our shackles were removed, we were locked up together in one of the big cages, and were called out in alphabetical groups of three to get our new wardrobes. Socks and underwear were first; used, but apparently freshly laundered. Every inmate gets 34"-36" cotton jockey-style underwear. If you are bigger than that, they are tight. If you are smaller, they are loose. Later on, once we got into our second level of cell block residences, we were able to select our own underwear out of a pile, if we moved quickly on the way to our showers, and there was a surprising range of elasticity among ones which had started out identical many wearings and washings earlier.

Undershirts were all Extra-Large, but they achieved a wide dissimilarity through use, abuse and laundering. It seems that none were ever thrown away. Stockings were cotton tube socks, without a heel. They had generally been worn enough times to have attained a vaguely foot-shaped contour.

A guard handed out the navy blue coveralls and the canvas shoes through a French door in a supply room. We had a choice in coveralls of small, medium, large or 3X. I took a large suit and a pair of size 10 shoes and went back into the cage to put them on. The suit turned out to be enormous. I was sure that a sumo wrestler had preceded me in incarceration. I didn't want to complain and make waves 24 hours into my years of imprisonment, but neither did I want to swim in my coveralls. I called over to the clothing cop and was let out of the cage to try again. I got a decent fit the second time.

The clothes do indeed make the man, psychologically as well as physically. In clean white underclothes, brand new black Converse shoes, and fitting, if frayed, blue coveralls, I felt like I belonged on the cover of GQ.

Next, we were called out for pictures and ID cards. The men with beards and/ or mustaches were required to shave them off with a cheap single-blade razor and no shaving cream. I had nothing to shave, but noises from those who did told me that it hurt like hell. A strange, but not surprising, thing was that the officials would take an inmate's photo *before* he shaved, with the result that the picture that he wore on his chest looked nothing like him, unless and until he grew back his foliage. Ace Wilson, an older biker type whom I would soon meet, came into the system with a ZZ Tops, waist-length beard, which he carried on his ID picture, while in person he looked like a clean shaven senator. I have asked why this and similarly irrational things are done, but have never received a sensible answer to any of my questions. You soon find out that rationality is not a long suit in the prison bureaucracy. Public employment is first and finally the basic consideration, so anything that necessitates a duplication of functions is a good, not an evil.

My photograph was slightly out of focus on the left side, as if I wasn't facing the camera straight on and that side was farther from the lens. It made me appear just a bit deformed, or perhaps as if I had had a stroke on that side. I definitely looked older on the left side. I had to live with it for a long time.

The ID cards had a hardy little metal clip attached to a plastic strap, which was strung through a horizontal slot at the top of the hard plastic cover. Throughout my years of imprisonment, the card would be with me constantly, clipped to my outer garment, chest high on the left side. Serious consequences would result from being caught without it, except when in bed, where it spent the night clipped to a bed post. If we went to the bathroom outside of our house during the night, we had to put it back on for the trip down the hall. I made it through three years of confinement without making that mistake of getting caught without my badge. When I eventually went to Work Release for the last five months of my sentence, where we were not required to wear an ID badge, it took me weeks to get over the feeling of nakedness, and I grabbed my chest whenever I saw an official.

In addition to my picture, the ID card had my name in capital letters, last name first, with "INMATE" below that in red capitals, next to which was my Department of Corrections number, 784783. Then:

Hair   Brown   Height 5'10"
Eyes   Gray   Weight 185
DOB   6/20/40
State of Washington
Department of Corrections
[BAR CODE]
Issued: 11/03/1998

A bar code! The ultimate stroke of dehumanization! I was as significant as a box of corn flakes! Everything there was to know about me could be viewed on a computer screen by scanning my barcode.

The plastic strap could be snapped open to admit additional cards for various purposes, which hung down vertically behind the ID. In effect, that was my wallet, except that it didn't carry money or condoms. Eventually, after some months, I would be adorned with an additional bright red card which represented a $5.00 per calendar quarter payment for the use of the weight room. A weight room card is something of a status symbol in the prison environment, especially for an older inmate. It subtly says, "DON'T FUCK WITH ME!"

As we sat in the cage, the men chattered away, especially the black guys. I was to quickly discover that black men in prison are very loud, which was not the experience that I had in many years of attendance at a black church. It was part of the prison conversational style for them to shout at each other in a normal conversation that did not seem to call for shouting.

A discussion was underway about the legal system, and the motivations of the people at the top. The consensus was that the criminal laws have been expanded to increase prison construction and prison employment. One of the social philosophers in the seminar offered his observations:

> "You know, the motherfuckers have taken a part of grow'in up and made it a fucking *felony*! Know what I'm sayin'? When we were in school back in the day, it was cool to bump some kid for his coat or his lunch. It was part of fucking grow 'in up! Know what I'm sayin'? Now the motherfuckers have taken a part of grow'in up and turned it into Second Degree fucking robbery! Know what I'm sayin'? Just to fill up this fucking place! That's fucking why!"

Dressed out and labeled, we were each given a slip of paper with a letter/number combination on it, indicating our new residence sections and cell numbers. Mine was "R-4, E-6", which of course meant nothing to me at the time. We were led out a doorway. On the way out, each of us picked up a bedroll, containing two sheets and a pillow case and a towel, rolled up in two dark blue wool Navy blankets that had a worn, much washed feeling to them. The quality of the linen had not improved from that of King County Jail. I also received my first "Chain Lunch", a brown bag with two sandwiches on stiff white bread, one with a smear of peanut butter and jelly between the unbuttered slices, and one with a shred of processed animal flesh, the "Mystery Meat" that I would come to know so well. No butter, mayo or mustard. Certainly no lettuce.

Over time, I periodically drew chain lunches when I fell into some function that blanked out a regular meal. Sometimes they included a foil-wrapped cookie or fruitless fruit bar of the Trail Meal type. I came to call the main course "Sandwich with an Attitude". It requires a malicious intent to make such a lousy sandwich. It seems like the worst, laziest inmates get the job of making chain lunches, and they rush through the early morning job as fast as they can.

A notable exception in bag lunches was in the meal that would be handed to us after dental appointments at the Washington Reformatory at Clallam Bay, on the tip of the Olympic Peninsula, where I had some tooth repair done on a couple of occasions in later years. We had to be transported some forty miles (without chains!) from our forest work camp, where there was no dentist. Clallam Bay is a nasty, hard time prison for higher risk convicts. We really got a feel for the Alcatraz kind of atmosphere when we were there. Security was oppressive, and it took at least two strip and body cavity searches to get in and out of the place. The wooden benches that we sat on in the dental waiting area, without even the old, dog-eared magazines that you get in the worst dentist's office in normal life, conditioned me to never again complain about a dentist's waiting room. But, after treatment, we were given sack lunches with sandwiches that were made with what seemed to be the very best deli case sliced beef, the best beef that I had in my entire term of imprisonment. Of course, our mouths were usually too messed up by the dentist to permit us to enjoy the sandwiches, and we were prohibited from taking them back to our own house. But, there are ways.

Provisioned with our new clothing and bedding, we passed down steps at an intersection with an underground concrete tunnel which reached an equal distance of about 100 yards to our left and right. We turned right and were headed for the "R' Units".

Every offender sentenced to serve time in a penitentiary in Washington State, regardless of the type of crime he committed or the length of his sentence, enters the system at the Washington Corrections Center at Shelton, after being transported on the Chain from the county jail in the county of his sentencing. Persons who were arrested, jailed and tried without ever being released on bail are moved to the R Units immediately after their sentencing. Those like me, who were at liberty on bail or personal recognizance prior to their sentencing, must turn themselves in at the county jail, which, as I have described, is not necessarily as easy as it sounds. I had once had illusions about getting a ride directly to the facility where I was to serve my time, and walking in like come celebrity mobster. No deal.

Headed for the R Units, our little bank of thieves, forgers, drug dealers, murderers and probation violators moved through the damp, resonant concrete tube. Occasional buckets had been placed to catch the most persistent of the leaks from seams in the concrete overhead. We passed a huge glassed-in guard station as we came out of the tunnel, with banks of controls and lights of one sort or another.

Inside, I caught a glimpse of one of the largest people I have ever seen, a woman guard whom I would come to know as "The Whale".

The R Units are three pods of ultra maximum security confinement, to hold and process the widely varied mix of Washington State's incoming criminality. Each pod is like on of those microcosms that high school science classes put together in big glass jugs, with a self contained ecological system that sustains life without contact with the rest of the universe. The most dangerous killers are mixed indiscriminately with nonviolent forgers and drug dealers, so total, minute-to-minute observation and control is maintained. Not always successfully, as I was soon to learn painfully.

I reached R-4 with my bedroll and chain lunch. The unit was in a 3-level building. The walking hallway that I took to get there was on the ground floor, open to the outdoors, but separated from the open air by a chain link fence from floor to ceiling. The dining area, serving only R-4, was also on the ground level. Up a flight of stairs were four 10-cell tiers, stretching out in parallel from the corners of a large open area with doors to a guard's duty room and a couple of counselors' offices. An identical four-tier layout was another flight up. The four lower tiers were labeled A, B, C and D. The upper tiers were E, F, G and H. I was assigned to Cell No. 6 on E Tier, so my mailing address became:

> Nelson Christensen 784783
> Washington Corrections Center, R-4, E-6
> Shelton, Washington 98584

The Mail Policy required that this entire return address appear on all outgoing mail, or it wouldn't "out-go". No abbreviations were permitted, like "WCC" for Washington Corrections Center. This ensured that our loved ones' postmen knew that *their* loved ones were in prison. In addition, each outgoing letter from an inmate was stamped in the prison post office with a friendly notice to the public:

> THIS WAS MAILED BY AN INMATE
> CONFINED AT A WASHINGTON STATE
> DEPARTMENT OF CORRECTIONS FACILITY.
> ITS CONTENTS ARE UNCENSORED

Part of the punishment, I guess. It served no other function whatsoever.

The upper tiers in the R-4 unit had a five foot-wide walkway running in front of the cells, with a large open space outside the railing reaching to the tier below. It gave the setting a nice authenticity, in the style of hard-time prison movies.

Moving down the upper walkway, you could imagine yourself in Attica, or some other stir, with Cagney and Stallone as fellow cons. I couldn't see the cells on the lower tier from inside my cell, or the tier above, because they were directly below and above, but at night I could see the reflection of the lower cells in the windows of the outer wall. It was occasionally satisfying to be able to match a face with an annoying loud voice.

The tiers in R-4 were really tiers, in the fashion of classic prison interiors. However, throughout any prison system, any hallway through a living unit is called a tier, even if it is the hall in a minimum security unit of two-man rooms with unlocked doors.

The doorway from the duty area to E-Tier was secured by a heavy gate of steel bars. A guard opened it by inserting a big brass key into a keyhole inside a steel box on the wall, which itself required a key for admittance. There was a metallic "clank" as the cable system inside the door took up its slack, then the barrier rolled to its left.

I passed through, still carrying my bedroll and brown bag meal, and walked down the tier past a two-nozzle open shower room and five cells before coming to my new home, E-6. This home I would call "6 House". The cell door, which was a structural continuation of the barred front wall of the cubicle, was sliding open to my left as I arrived.

The first cellmate of my imprisonment, Mario, was standing in the room. He was a small Mexican man in his early thirties, smiling, and, in our brief acquaintance, painfully polite and considerate. He spoke only a few diffident words of English.

This opened an acquaintance with scores of Mexican men who served time with me, taught me some of their language and their songs, and made me a confirmed advocate of compulsory English language education. Nearly all of the Mexicans whom I came to know were unable to communicate in English at even an infantile level, often after having lived in the U.S. for many years. They generally didn't have much of an idea what had happened to them in the legal process. Throughout their incarceration, their illiteracy was nurtured by English-as-a Second-Language courses that never seemed to produce any recognizable results, and a penal system policy of anesthesyzing them with Mexican-language television. You think American TV programs are stupid? You should watch Mexican TV! But, lots of good looking women with big tits!

Mario anxiously rummaged through his property, all of which was held in a medium-sized brown paper bag, and pulled out several letters from the State of Washington workmen's' compensation officials, the general tenor of which was that his monthly compensation payments for a back injury were suspended pending a medical examination and report, which would of course be hard for him to get while he was in prison. After reading through the correspondence, I told him that I would help him write a letter the next day. When I came back from dinner a few hours later, Mario and his belongings were gone, and I never saw him again. I assume, with the knowledge that I later acquired regarding procedures in the R Units, that he had been in R-4 for a month or more, and had been moved on to R-5 or R-6, the last step before being shipped out on another Chain to a permanent institutional assignment. I had lost my first legal client in captivity, but he certainly would not be my last!

6

HOME ON THE TIER

There were ten cells on our tier, side-by-side, facing out toward a walkway and railing, beyond which was empty space dropping off to the tier below. We referred to our cells as "1 House", or whatever the number was. The mix of men was as diverse as could be. Nearly every race, personality and crime known to man was represented. We were fortunate to have only two men to a cell. When I came back through on a transfer between prison facilities some two years later, the place was so crowded that there were three men in many cells. Since there were only two bunks, new arrivals had to sleep and live on a mattress thrown on the floor. In prison slang, this person was known as "The Rug". The existence of a rug is miserable indeed, and the misery is shared somewhat by his cellies, as they must step over him whenever they move around in the cramped space. The normal lack of privacy in matters such as going to the toilet shrinks to a nothingness.

It is impossible to describe the social and psychological atmosphere that engulfed our tier of new arrivals. The place was awash in adrenaline, as twenty men started out on a new life of imprisonment. Many of the men had been here before, and many, especially among the black men, knew each other, were related or had common acquaintances on the streets. There was unremitting shouting between cells, and many men stood at the doors of their cells and bellowed constantly for no real reason other than to let off steam and, in some cases, apparently to establish a sort of rooster-in-the-barnyard prominence. The noise did not end at the ll:00 p.m. "lights out". For the first week I could not sleep, and my temper burned. To shout out, "shut up!" would bring a violent response, as if a First Amendment right was being challenged, and if the shouter was identified, there might be consequences in the Yard the next day. Eventually, after the first few weeks of imprisonment, I would achieve an ability to sleep on the stage of a rock concert. If prison did nothing else for me, after my release I would never have any trouble sleeping anywhere, in any noise.

One black man on the tier below stood at the front of his cell and shouted continuously through the bars at his homies in the upper and lower tiers, in a voice of thundering timbre and resonance. He *never* shut up. The other black inmates called him "The Screamin' Nigger". I didn't, but I sure agreed with the "screamin" part. Although he was out of my direct sight, being directly below me on the lower tier, I saw his reflection in the window at night. He had a distinctive "do", with his hair wound up in something like Mickey Mouse Ears. That enabled me to identify him when we were outside in the yard. I went up to him and said, "I sure do enjoy your work!" He stared at my in puzzlement. I guess I was lucky that my big mouth didn't get me a fist in the face. My luck wouldn't hold for long.

There was a particularly annoying man in 7 House, one up from mine. A white man about 35, he stood at the bars of his cell, night and day, loudly bragging about his criminal achievements and, particularly, his sexual experiences. You are forced to listen to a lot of demented sexual fantasies in prison. From what this guy said in his ramblings, it seemed to me that he had spent too much of his life in prison to have had very many sexual relationships, and, being tired of his bullshit, I told him so. I began to enjoy needling him. Being unable to see his face, since I couldn't see around the corner into his cell, I was unaware of the cold fury that I was building up in him. My mouth was going to cost me in the very near future.

Every once in a while, you will read in the newspaper about the police getting incriminating statements from a prisoner by planting a "ringer" in his cell. It always seemed to me that that would be quite a difficult task, and I would imagine the agent having to cleverly interrogate the subject. In fact, all you need is someone who can remember what the guy said. When they are first confined, criminals are charged-up motor mouths, who can't stop bragging to each other about their crimes and what the police were unable to discover. Very often, they still have crack cocaine or methamphetamines in their brains. They can't help spilling their guts.

After we returned to our cells from dinner on the first night on the tier, the loudspeaker announced the schedule for showers.

"Showers tonight for 1 House through 5 House! You have five minutes for showers!"

By this announcement, I learned that we would only get to shower and change underwear and socks every other day. Since I was in 6 House, today was not my day. Fortunately, I had taken a quick shower at King Count Jail that morning.

Nevertheless, in my normal life, a nice hot shower would have been the order of the day that evening.

The five minute limit for showers was no joke. You had to be standing naked and ready when your cell door slid open. You hustled down the walkway toward the two-nozzle shower room, located between the entry gate and 1 House, carrying your old towel and your dirty shorts, undershirt and socks, along with soap, and shampoo if you had it. The old towel and linen were thrown on a pile, and you hurried into the shower. Once you got the movements down, there was usually about 4 ½ minutes available for the shower, which is adequate for a quick one, without singing. When you came out, an inmate porter handed you a roll between the bars of the gate, consisting of a new towel, shorts, undershirt and socks. They were all used, of course, and one-size-fits-all, which can be pretty funny sometimes. There was seldom any elastic left in the shorts. Everything seemed to be clean but stained.

When we were ready to move on to our new destinations, usually after six weeks to two months, we would transfer into a new wing, either R-5 or R-6, which was about a quarter of a mile across the prison grounds. The shower routine was the same there, except that the replacement linen was piled loosely on tables. We could take a few seconds to select our own linen, so we could generally get a better fit than in the general issue. Not exactly shopping at Nordstrom, but little things mean a lot in stir!

My second cellie turned up the day after Mario's disappearance. He was Brent Jones, a 29-year-old white guy. We would get along well in our compressed environment for three weeks, until events to be related later separated us. Brent was a very resourceful young man, and a decent guy, by the unique standards of "decency" in prison. He had been a sergeant in the Army Special Forces, serving in Panama, and had a military orderliness and cleanliness that makes for a good cellie. He would manufacture living aids, like a toilet paper roll holder and a towel rack, out of the few raw materials that we had—rubber bands, one large paper bag each, pencil stubs and a couple of Post-its. Brent had been an accomplished methamphetamine manufacturer, an occupation that requires precision if you are to keep from blowing yourself up He described the manufacturing and distribution process to me in exacting detail. He said,

"I love the way meth customers stick with you. One hit and you own them for life."

He fit a pattern that I was to discern over the years, that meth is almost exclusively a white people's drug, while crack cocaine is pretty much a black thing. In three years, I never met a black man who had had any experience with meth, although most of them were doing time for drug related offenses. It may be the expense. A meth habit is *very* expensive.

I will never again know such a possession-free life. My entire wardrobe consisted of a pair of threadbare navy blue coveralls, a cotton undershirt and jockey shorts, rubber shower shoes, low-cut Converse tennis shoes and a pair of socks. I had one thin towel. My toilet kit was a toothbrush and small comb, a Motel Six bar of soap, a tiny tube of toothpaste and a disposable single blade BIC razor. Everything I owned was kept in a brown paper bag, placed on the floor under the bunk bed.

One day we got a new guy on the tier who was different from anyone else there. His name was Rex. Actually, I think that was a nickname. He was a recent migrant to Seattle from Detroit. A different breed of cat! Seattle criminals are, like everyone else in Seattle, polite and accommodating, with some sense of the boundaries of decency under their criminality. This guy was different. He was a Bad Dude! 24 years old, he was about 5' 7" tall and was just as wide, with no fat. A black assault vehicle.

I found myself talking to Rex in the Yard. He approached me after someone told him that I was a lawyer. He felt that he had been wrongfully sentenced above the sentencing guidelines, and that his 47-year sentence was too long. I listened to his story and told him that I would do some research if I got access to the prison's law library. At that point, I was not too hot on criminal law, which had never been a specialty in my practice. Boy, would that change over the next three years!

Rex told me that in his drug world in Detroit, he and his associates would take over and terrorize an entire residential high rise in the projects as their business location. Customers would come and go openly. A K-Mart of crack! Criminal guards manned the roof with rifles. If the cops came, the guards would shoot at them from above, safe from return fire. The cops would split, giving the bad guys a chance to go on with their business or disappear.

It was a world of flaming violence, not just between cops and robbers, but often between the robbers themselves. Territorial disputes, fueled by cocaine paranoia, created a constant threat of violent death. Rex accumulated too many enemies for his own peace of mind and he decided to get out of Detroit. Like many Easterners, he had heard that Seattle was a nice place to live, so he and his lady headed West. He got there and established himself in his old business and was doing well. But, one night he was stopped by a Seattle patrolman. The officer came up and shined his flashlight in the driver's window.

Still acting on his old Detroit instincts, Rex shot him. Fortunately for all concerned, the officer lived. Unfortunately for Rex, there are especially persuasive interrogation techniques for people who shoot police officers. Getting out of the Seattle City Jail and into the county lockup was a great relief to Rex.

When Rex told his story in prison, the reaction was uniform among the armed robbers, drug dealers, and even the murderers.

"You shot a fucking cop! Jesus Christ! You don't shoot cops!"

Seattle nice.

Rex Shrugged. "Hey! The motherfucker was in my face! Know what I'm sayin'?"

Rex was the first black man who I saw with the Gangster Walk that you read about but only see a feeble imitation of imitation of in Seattle. It is a rolling, threatening embodiment of *attitude*. One foot swings out and forward, not just forward as in a normal stride. The heel angles downward, the toes up and slightly out. The opposite shoulder dips down and back. The foot lands, heel first, and that shoulder rolls forward. The opposite foot swings out and forward to start the second half of the cycle. The arms hang slightly curved, with swinging hands curled into a half fist. Sometimes the hands are folded in front of the chest, for a particularly authoritative effect. The head moves independently, connected to the walk only in rhythm. It bobs slightly up and down in a knowing, threatening coolness as the scene is taken in. Rex, a lion stalking through the Serengeti!

I struck up a conversation in the Big Yard with an older guy, at least "older" in the largely youthful fraternity that we were in. He was walking around the track in a daze, an appearance that had earned him the nickname "Rain Man", after the Dustin Hoffman movie character.

His name was John, and he was 47 years old, but he seemed older than my 58 years, because of his graying hair and his slow, sleepy manner. He was doing 48 months for Attempted Murder. He had intended to suffocate his father with a pillow. The old man was dying of cancer in a hospice and was suffering a lot on his way out. John decided to do a Kevorkian on him and hurry him on his way, a decision with its own pain. He changed his mind after pressing the pillow down on his father's face, not so much from a change of intention as from the inability to sustain his resolve through what was turning out to be a horrific experience. It would have been one thing to hold yourself together through the split second that it takes to pull the trigger of a gun; quite another to spend long minutes squeezing the life out of a human being, your own father!

As it happened, John pulled the pillow off of his father's face seconds after a nurse started watching him from the door of the room. She reported the incident, and a zealous prosecuting attorney charged him with attempted murder. The old man died of his cancer three days after the incident.

The trauma of the whole scenario pretty much took John apart. One day he was a proud, comfortable cabinet maker, and the next he was a prisoner charged with a felony, and, further, a prisoner of his own thoughts. He was dosed up with lithium all the time, which caused his Rain Man appearance. I was surprised to see him a few weeks later, off the lithium, and he was striding purposefully across the dining area.

The whole story came to me from John, and on the basis of later experience I don't know whether I should have believed him or not. I eventually learned that many inmates who had committed crimes which were embarrassing even among criminals invented new crimes for themselves. This was almost universally the case when it came to sex crimes, especially child molestation crimes.

7

"BEND OVER, PLEASE!"

In the first day or so in our residence, we were sent in groups of ten to have our entrance physicals. Adams, the chief cop in the eating area, of whom more later, made a big deal out of the prostate prospect when he announced at breakfast the names of those who were to go directly to the infirmary after the meal. As he announced each name, he smiled and pointed an index finger toward the ceiling, as if the finger was entering someone's butt.

We walked through the concrete tunnel to the infirmary and waited outside the entry in a fairly decent room with upholstered furniture. There was a guard inside a glass cage, with a big Space Station consol in front of her. When you were permitted entry, she pulled a bunch of levers and the big steel door rolled open.

The physical was rudimentary. Mostly a matching up of inmates with records, if any, that had been forwarded with the inmate, and the taking of a brief medical history.

"Any accidents or injuries since you arrived? How do you feel today?"

The record of the examination of the chemical burn on my foot had followed me, and I was sent into a nurse to have it examined and dressed. A daily visit was placed in my schedule, which gave me a nice break from the cell for a couple of weeks. As has been said by every person who ever wrote about the prison experience, a visit to a medical facility is invariably a brief journey through the looking glass to a place of relative dignity.

The feared prostate examination did not happen to everyone. Only I, being much older than the rest of my colleagues, was called in for a prostate exam. An actual medical doctor, which is something that you almost never meet in prison—a nurse practitioner is generally the most advanced care giver, for everything short of heart surgery—came out and asked me into his office. I went into a large, well appointed room, and he asked me to sit down while he reviewed my file. He commented, "Oh, I see you are a lawyer." Then he directed me to the "bend-over table" that some genius designed for prostate exams.

I was familiar with the procedure, having been through it many times over the years, and I wasn't at all apprehensive about it. Hell! In prison, unless you cross the line, it's as close to sex as you get! (Two and a half years later, a female nurse practitioner, who was giving me the exam, said, "Nice prostate!" I have to say, that's about the greatest praise I have ever had from any woman about that area of my anatomy!)

I did what I was told to do, and the doctor did what he was supposed to do. However, while he had his arm inside me up to his elbow—at least it felt that way—he said,

"Do you mind if I ask you a personal question?"

Well, I thought, we were pretty good friends by then, so I said, "Uh!! Fine!", thinking, what in the hell is he going to ask me? Is this the start of a beautiful affair?

After he finished, all of the cleanup was over, and my pants were back up around my waist, he sat at his desk and motioned for me to sit down. He looked at me very seriously and said,

"You are a lawyer, right?"

"Right", I replied.

"Tell me. Are those lawyer shows on television realistic? Like Allie McBeal?"

I knew that he wanted to believe.

"Yeah," I said. "They're just like real life!"

8

"YOUR TABLE IS READY"

The legendary bottom line benefit of imprisonment is that you get "Three Hots and a Cot." The Hots are breakfast, lunch and dinner, and their temperature, as well as their general palatability, varies vastly from institution to institution. And sometimes you only get "Two Hots" in a day, not three, on weekends. The Cot is, of course, your bunk, which is always there for you.

Our pod of eight tiers in the R Units included its own dining room within the same ultra secure enclosure. The tiers were called for meals two at a time, 30 minutes apart. Five minutes to get there, twenty minutes to eat and clear your gear, and five minutes to get back into your cell. That is not a lot of time to walk the length of the tier, go down two flights of stairs, snail through the service line and make the return trip up the stairs and down the length of the tier, sandwiching (no pun intended!) a meal between the movements.

My first dinner came at 4:00 p.m. on my day of arrival. That's early for dinner, in my life experience, but once body and mind are locked into the constant, unvarying clockwork of prison life, Pavlovian triggers are installed in the unconscious. The low rumble of cell doors rolling open on the tier below tells the mind that food comes in a half hour, and saliva and digestive juices start to flow.

The menu the first night was liver and onions (This was, after all, supposed to be punishment), baked potato and green beans. With strawberry shortcake for desert! I was cautioned against too much positive reaction to the desert by memory of the story of the guy who died and went to Hell, where he saw everyone waist-deep in a river of shit, drinking Starbucks coffee. He thought, "This isn't going to be too bad". Then the Devil shouted, "All right! Coffee break is over! Everyone back down!"

The strawberry shortcake was a nice piece of comedy. A guard stood behind the inmate who was serving up the strawberries. I learned over time that there was always a cop present whenever something particularly good was being served. The strawberries, mashed into a thick syrup, were served, one portion per diner,

46

from a tiny, two-tablespoon ladle. The server, who was enjoying his temporary power, would say to each unhappy recipient of the meager dole,

"I know! I know! You'll see me in the yard!"

At the end of the brief line we passed into another small room holding twenty round, four-man tables. The tables were of prison design, bolted to the floor, with circular, backless seats attached by rivets to the central trunk of the table. All steel. Nothing to pick up and throw or swing.

Two tiers of inmates eating at one time filled the room. Three officers stood watch at the door. One, Adams, became a dominating figure in every inmate's life, for the weeks that the inmate lived in the pod. Adams' purpose in life was to move us through the dining process, in and completely out the door, in the 15-20 minutes allotted. He roared constantly, in a big, bullhorn voice:

"Don't stare at it! Eat it!"

"Mr. Weiner is to eat, not to play with!"

We learned to eat a meal without ever having a hand free of a utensil, because the minute your hands were free, Adams was over you pressuring you to clear out.

Surprisingly, in the grim, ironic humor of prison, Adams was regarded as a "upper" in the psychological atmosphere of the day, partly because he was a cartoon caricature of the legendary brutal prison guard. More so, because he knew it and in fact obviously manufactured the persona for its practical, if comic, effect.

The food in the entry R Units was surprisingly good, if not great, especially considering the circumstances of its preparation and presentation. Everything was cooked in a central kitchen, and was served to the entire prison, wherever the eaters might be. Long-term inmate population, a quarter mile away, and transients who had moved on to the departure units, ate in a large dining hall, to which they walked over outdoor sidewalks from their units. We ate the same food that they we ate in the entry R Units. However, ours came to our unit in serving pans in heated carts on wheels, or in unheated pans for salads, Jell-O, etc. And it was generally well presented and palatable, if not succulent. Our food was served by inmates on a serving line, and we held out a tray and they slapped something on it, just like Stallone got in the movie. In the main dining hall, with "live" food, the filled tray came through a window as you walked past in a line. No chance to get a little favor from an inmate server who might owe you one.

The food was usually guarded in its journey by The Whale, the truly enormous woman copy who I had seen in the guard station. She must have stolen a large portion of it on the way. I have, seriously, never seen a bigger functional human being in my life. She had to weight at least 600 pounds. It was all the more impressive that she always wore a perfectly tailored uniform. I envisioned a crane lowering it over her body in the morning.

I had only been in prison for three weeks when Thanksgiving, 1998, came along. Thanksgiving dinner had turkey, stuffing, cranberries, and all of the other essentials, and wasn't bad.

9

"YOUR PAPERS, PLEASE!"

"Christensen, in Six House! Report to the Duty Station!"

The instruction blared over the p.a. system, and the door of my cell rolled open. I stepped out and walked down the tier to the big gate. It rolled open as I approached. On the other side one of the guards stood waiting for me.

"Christensen! Has anyone asked to see you paperwork?"

"What's paperwork?", I replied.

He gave me a look of disgust at my stupidity. I was such a novice in the system that I didn't know one of the most basic terms of prison lingo.

"Your paperwork! Your Judgment and Sentence that shows what crimes you were sentenced for!"

I told him that I didn't have any of that stuff with me, that I had not brought any of my legal papers with me when I checked in the King County Jail. Thinking back a few days, I remembered my puzzlement when I saw that some inmates carried boxes of legal papers through the admissions system, the only personal possessions that they were permitted to keep. Having been stung a few time for denying inmates their legal rights, the system bent over backwards to give form, if not substance, to legal empowerment. I would eventually learn that there are some guys, even ones with very long sentences, who are always working on appeals and petitions. As my prison legal practice grew, I would get involved in many of those actions, with mixed success.

I told the guard that no one had asked for my paperwork.

"Why would anyone care about that?", I asked him.

"Because there is a rumor on one of the tiers that you're a lily shaker", he replied.

I *did* know what a lily shaker was, from my experience as a lawyer. A lily shaker is a sexual exhibitionist and/or a child molester! I have never molested anyone but grown women, and always with what I, at least, regarded as at least a modicum of consent.

"Why does anyone think I'm a lily shaker?", I asked him.

"Because that's usually what clean-cut, middle aged guys are in here for."

Jesus! The last thing in the world I needed in the prison environment was for a rumor to get around that I was a child molester! Which I wasn't! I was a doing time for wrongful sale of securities and theft, good old red blooded American crimes!

Child molesters and rapists serve very uncomfortable time in prisons. One man who worked on the serving line in the kitchen was said to be a child molester, and my cellie, who came from the same county, confirmed the accusation. As the rumor grew, the guy disappeared. He had been "PC'd up", which meant that he had asked to be swept into protective custody. Of course, that put him in with the tender young men who had been PC'd up to protect them from predators, so maybe the system turned back on itself!

"Don't throw me in the briar patch!"

There is a Holier than Thou mindset among convicts, which extends to foreign spies as well, that enables them to posture as "I'm not *that* bad!" good guys. Perhaps, too, there is legitimate everyman contempt for such wrongdoers. In any event, the chance of getting beat up or killed in prison is enhanced tremendously by being labeled as a child molester. Even short of violence, the inmate so labeled is marginalized and kept out of the everyday social loop that is necessary to easy time. However, I would prove capable of getting beat up on my own merits!

I could tell by his manner that the guard was suspicious of me and would himself like to see my paper work. I told him that I was not a child molester, but a good, honest thief, and that no one had asked to see my paperwork. Actually, since the rumors came from another tier, with whose occupants I would have very little contact, there wasn't much chance that I would be asked, although it might happen in the yard during recreation, where I could conveniently be beaten up.

The guard sent me back to my cell. Some unseen hand pushed buttons, and the necessary gates rolled open. At the next recreation period, I stood in line for a phone to send out an urgent request for a copy of my Judgment and Sentence. I knew that I could not reach my attorney through the complicated collect-call system that costs the recipient of prisoner calls a fortune. Instead, I called my daughter in New York, whom I could always reach at her job at a television network. I asked her to call my attorney and tell him to send my Judgment and Sentence *ASAP!* It arrived in the mail two days later. I made a point of showing it to as many people as I could, and quickly became somewhat legendary for the apparent scope and sophistication of my crimes. The fact that my wrongdoing deprived my victims of something over half a million dollars set me aside from the penny ante felons around me. Standards of distinction are different in prison. I used to good naturedly scorn one of my cellies, a young man who had carjacked a Toyota in a discount mall.

"I'm so ashamed to live with someone who stole a *Toyota* from in front of a Nordstrom Rack!", I would moan.

Although he knew I was joking, he shared my shame.

Anyway, the word got around that my paperwork showed that I was not a lily shaker, and my image in society stayed high.

10

HOME SWEET HOME

My Cell is seven feet wide, eleven feet deep and eight feet high, a space that I share with a temporarily retired methamphetamine dealer. The floor is concrete. The walls and ceiling are painted a flat gray. A Benjamin Moore color wheel might call it "Volcanic Ash".

The front wall of the room consists of nineteen vertical steel bars, each an inch thick. They are spaced five inches apart, and continue through the two-foot-wide door which is inserted one foot from the left side of the room, looking out. The bars are fitted through holes in one-foot-by-three-inch steel strips, lying crosswise at one-foot vertical intervals, to keep the vertical bars from being parted, Samson style. The door opens and closes sideways on rollers, at the whim of a guard who operates the governing mechanism, who is located five identical cells and a shower stall to the right of mine, looking in. There must be an elliptical cable arrangement that enables the operator to engage one or more of the doors, including four past mine, at the same time.

When an occupant of a single cell is called out for an event exclusive to him, his door can be opened alone. For facility-wide functions, such as meals, indoctrination or group exercise, all of the doors can be opened in a nearly simultaneous series. On such occasions, it sounds like a freight train starting up from a dead stop, as the slack in the cable between the successive doors takes up. CLANK! Hmmm…CLANK! Hmmm…CLANK! Hmmm….

A third of the width of my cell, on the right side, looking out, is taken up by two bunks, top and bottom. Each bunk is a two-foot by six-foot steel plate, welded inside a rectangular steel flange with a two-inch vertical lip, to hold in the mattress. Each assembly is attached at one end to the rear wall, apparently by bolts from the outside, since there are no bolts showing. The front end rests on triangular steel braces, which are bolted to the side wall. The standard issue mattress, which is identical from institution to institution, is a heavy plastic envelope filled with a state-of-the-art material which spontaneously forms baseball-size tumors. Two thin sheets and a pillow case, a small, bumpy pillow, and two good Navy wool blankets round out the sleeping kit.

All of the cells other than mine, at least the ones I have seen while walking down the tier, have a small steel desk bolted to the wall across from the bunks. Mine was apparently ripped off the wall by a formidable former resident, leaving three holes that evidence the past presence of three very substantial bolts. The wall has been painted without repairing the holes. The repair job probably falls in the bureaucratic crack between plasterer and painter. Prep doesn't appear to be a big consideration in government painting.

In such a small space, there is of course no closet or armoire. This isn't a problem, since my cellie and I each only have a towel and a pair of coveralls to hang up. To accommodate these, there are two "hangers" on the wall across from the bunks. The first is fifteen inches back from the bars, the other a foot farther back. Each consists of a foot-long steel strip, ¼ inch thick, hanging vertically, with the bottom end turned up in a rough hook, four feet from the floor. Each assembly is attached to the wall with two bolts with one-inch hexagonal heads. No telling how long the bolts are, but my experience with such things tells me that they have to be at least six inches long, with such massive heads. Suffice it to say, they should be sufficient to support my towel and coveralls.

Two feet above and a foot to the rear of the aft hanger is what was apparently designed as a bookshelf. It is a steel plate, protruding nine inches from the wall, with flanges on each end five inches high at the wall, sloping down triangularly to meet the front corners at the base. Just as I never needed a wine cellar because I always drank the wine as soon as I bought it, we don't need a book shelf because each book that we can lay our hands on is hungrily and immediately consumed when it enters our cell, then passed on to eager neighbors. Consequently, book shelves serve as a platform for such toiletries as we have, currently a toothbrush, a small tube of toothpaste, a bar of soap and a disposable single blade razor each. We are also permitted to wedge a photograph of a loved one behind the end of the shelf, up to 8"x 10". Neither of us yet has any pictures.

Fit into the space where the wall meets the ceiling above the book shelf/medicine cabinet is a steel casing containing a standard four-foot, two-tube fluorescent light fixture, and, at the rear end of the ceiling, a radio speaker with no volume control. The light fixture is covered with translucent plastic, on top of which are steel crosshatches It is the sole, but adequate, source of artificial light in the room. The radio speaker plays FM stations selected by management. There is, however, intense lobbying by competing ethnic groups for station selection. Not much call for country music, since most of the white inmates are young, urban drug dealers.

They usually vote with the black men. Voting is done by shouting something like, "Change the motherfucking station!" The blacks, being the most vocal and loudest, as well as the most numerous, usually prevail. Sometimes the Mexicans get a sop thrown to them. It seems that only I and the guards care for country music. When the radio comes on at 5:30 a.m., it is usually country, and that stays on until the hip hop voters get their voices warmed up.

On the back wall, a few inches from the outer edge of the top bunk, a metal mirror is riveted to the wall. A history of abuse has left it scratched and foggy, so that it is virtually worthless. But good enough for combing your hair, and I so seldom have to tie a necktie.

Mounted on the back wall, a foot from the wall across from the bunks is our most prominent piece of furniture: a one-piece stainless steel combination toilet and sink, designed as an instrument of our punishment. There is no moveable seat on the toilet. The seat is molded into the body. This is objectionable, on one hand, because we suffer the same offense that women who live with men have always suffered. Males passing water while standing up, as permitted by our unique configuration, inevitably hit or splash the seat. This gives rise in the prison environment to an inflexible rule that a wipe-off of the stationary seat with a wet tissue or paper towel follow every peeing. (This "inflexible rule" was, as I have described, relaxed in the dormitory cell that I occupied in the King County Jail, where there were two toilets, respectively labeled "Shitter" and "Pisser".

There is a compensatory advantage to the seatless toilet for males who have been scolded throughout their lives by mothers, lovers and wives for not "lifting the seat". Here, both the scold and the seat are absent, so there is certain liberation in the prison environment.

Above the toilet, in the same stainless steel casing, is a 10" by 8" sink. A simple water spout that squirts faintly upward is activated by unlabeled hot and cold metal buttons that produce water only while a strong force is being applied to them. Since there is no stopper in the sink, all ablutions must be performed with one hand, while the other presses the button. The water is either hot or cold, never a comfortable combination of the two, since it cannot be mixed without pushing both buttons at the same time, which would leave no hand free for operations.

There is a cylindrical hole in the side of the structure, on your right when you are sitting down, to hold a role of toilet paper. Experience quickly teaches that the roll gets soggy from spilled water if it is left there, so we set the roll on the floor under the lower bunk, within reach but out of harm's way.

In spite of its eccentricities, the toilet does work, and it works quite well, mechanically speaking. It flushes with a "Whoosh!!!", and I think that it would swallow a watermelon without gulping. I am wakened many times each night by flushings along the tier, but I suspect that I will get used to the sound, like you eventually get used to the 3:00 a.m. train when you live next to the railroad tracks.

Privacy is checked at the gate of the first penal institution that you enter in a term of imprisonment. Toilets in a cell are always out in the open in high security stir. No stalls, no doors. In a multi-person cell, a certain etiquette develops. When my cellie suggests that he needs to occupy the toilet, I sit on the front end of my bunk and read, or whatever I'm doing, facing out toward the bars. If he is going to be there a while, he flushes continually to keep the atmosphere as friendly as possible. The ritual is followed in all cells, an unspoken part of the social contract. The leisurely trip to the bathroom with the sports page and a cup of coffee is gone, a typical element of the mass of small deprivations that constitute the essence of the penal experience. There are some private bathrooms in out-of-the-way places like the hospital, and a visit there is an occasion for a rare private experience.

It's hard to imagine it being by intentional design, but also hard to think that it's overlooked, that the space between my cell and the adjoining cells is only about one foot wide, enabling us to easily pass items from cell to cell. In the evening, a thriving flea market hums through this throat of commerce. Books, coffee, toiletries, spare linen, contraband tobacco. As another part of the social contract, an item can be set forth from "10 House" with instructions for it to be passed to "1 House" with confidence that it will complete its journey. Honor among thieves. However, a bar of soap will make it a lot faster than a sports page or a National Enquirer!

Because we are a mixed bag of murderers, forgers, thieves, rapists, burglars and what-have-you, this is a maximum security facility. Except for meals and an hour two of "Yard", which is what recreation is called, whether it is in the outside yard or in the gym, we are locked down in our cells 24 hours a day. "24-7", as they say on the streets. But as the old song says, "It takes a heap of living to make a house a home".

11

I GET MY JUST DESSERTS

The day before I reported to start serving my time in prison, Glen, my friend of forty years, said to me:

"Nelson, I have one word of advice for you. Your mouth. If anything is going to get you in trouble in prison, it will be your mouth. I've known you too long."

I should have listened. My smart-ass lawyer's mouth was not well suited to the prison environment.

The noisy braggart in 7-House next to me was getting on my nerves. His name was James Zimmerman. About 37 years old. He had long, straight black hair and the rough face of tough living. Kind of a biker look. He was one of those stir-crazy jerks who have been in half the county jails west of Omaha, and a good number of the prisons. Most of his last 15 years had been spent under lock and key.

Day and night, Zimmerman stood at the bars of his cell babbling in a loud, annoying voice about his sexual exploits. In prison, it's always possible for some-one like that to get a couple other sexually twisted idiots to join in a "Can you top this?" sex slam. If it's Black men, the reference to the female sexual partner is always "the bitch".

"Then I rolled the bitch over and stuck it to her! The bitch loved it!"

For the white men, the terminology is equally degrading, and the descriptions are uniformly sick. Strange how guys who have been in prison most of their adult lives could have so much wild sex!

With Zimmerman orchestrating it, this crap went on nonstop late into the night, every night. If no one else wanted to play, he would go on by himself. I was sick and tired of Zimmerman.

I was cool. Do your own time. I had learned from listening that it doesn't do any good to tell one these guys to shut up. It just jacks up their adrenaline. So, I was cool.

Until about the third week. I was alone in my house. My cellie, Jones, was on Sergeant's Crew, a posh gig that kept him out on the property most of the day. I was dozing on my bunk a couple hours before dinner, when Nate, Zimmerman's cellie in 7 House, called my name. Nate and my cellie were homies from Clallam County. They shared things, including a jar of Nes Café instant coffee that Jones kept in our house. It had to be mixed with tap water, which was only slightly warm, but bad coffee is sometimes better than no coffee at all. (This was the beginning of my five years of bad coffee!). Nate was always asking for some of the coffee, and when he did, he handed a paper cup around the wall to where it could be grabbed by one of us. We would put some coffee powder in it and hand it back. Simple, except that it was against rules for inmates to share or loan anything.

I consistently refused to pass tobacco, which was the most common commodity in commerce on the tier. There was a tobacco tolerance by the guards, who knew what was going on. But the penalty on the books for possession of tobacco was stiff—48 hours in the Hole and 10 days loss of "Good Time". They could come down on you if they wanted. I stayed out of that loop totally.

Coffee was something else. It was legal to have it. They sold it on Store. It was the sharing or loaning of it that was prohibited. You only got a few penalty points on your card for passing it, but points eventually lead to an infraction, which can send you to the Hole and cost you Good Time. Still, to avoid being a complete goody-goody jerk, which can lose you the basic good will among the population that gets you essential cooperation in the small things of life, I passed coffee.

I got up when Nate called. Parenthetically, it must be noted that I am always in a very bad mood—nasty as a rattlesnake—when I wake up from a nap. As my time in prison progressed, this was a very significant trait that I had to deal with.

Nate's cup appeared in a hand outside the bars. I put coffee in it and was about to hand it back through the bars when I looked up and there was a guard standing there, having apparently approached from the direction of 7 House. I was handing the cup to the guard!

There may have been a tolerance policy for passing coffee, but tolerance has to thin out when you do it right in front of a cop! Fortunately, I hadn't put the cup through the bars and was able to smile a weak smile and fake a drink from the cup. The guard smiled, and that was all there was to it. But I knew that a few more inches of movement of the cup would have force his hand.

I was pissed, enhanced in good part by my post-nap nastiness and by my general hostility toward Zimmerman. I took off on 7 House.

"You assholes! You set me up! You knew there was a cop on the tier and you set me up. Keep your fucking games to yourselves, and don't ever talk to me! And it would be great if Zimmerman would quit his fucking jabbering and you two just sit there and jack each other off!"

Don't take your guns to town, son....

As I said, I am pretty nasty when I wake up from a nap.

A rare silence fell over the tier. Eventually there were a few soft exclamations of, "Wow!" and "Heavy!" from unidentified cells. Someone who recognized my voice said, "The old man really erupted!"

I sat back on my bunk and tried to read, but I was really wound up. By the time I calmed down a bit, mainline for dinner was called, and the cell doors rolled open. I laid down my book and stood up. Suddenly I saw that Zimmerman was standing a couple of feet inside my house! You *never* go into someone else's house! More than a breach of courtesy, it is a major disciplinary infraction.

It wasn't possible to tell from his face if Zimmerman was angry. He always looked angry. But his mood quickly became apparent.

"You're calling me a fucking snitch? You can fucking apologize now!"

I said, "Get out of my house!"

WHAP!!!!

I had a brief glimpse of his right fist swinging over and down, but no time to avoid it. He caught me on the left side of my head, just in the corner of my eye. I spun around and landed face down on my bunk. I put my hand to my head and it came away covered with blood. I got up and grabbed my towel—my only towel—from the hook on the opposite wall, leaving a path of blood across the floor. Zimmerman was gone.

I wet the towel in the sink and dabbed my face with it. The bleeding wouldn't stop. I think I read somewhere about skin wounds to the face being especially bad bleeders. My towel looked like it had cleaned up after the Manson Family. In retrospect, I certainly wasn't thinking as clearly as I thought I was at the time, but I realized that I had to do something quickly. This being prison, you don't want to snitch. If you rat on another inmate, even one who had slugged you, the environment can get unpleasant, even if sentiment in the population lines up with you over the incident. All things considered, it's always advisable to keep problems among the inmates and not involve the cops. Situations work themselves out eventually within the convict social/legal system.

I knew that a guard would come down the tier any second to see that the inmates had all cleared out to dinner. If I somehow avoided his view, I still would be missing at the check-in at dinner. Eating wasn't compulsory, but showing up was.

In a few seconds my cell door and the gate at the end of the tier would close, trapping me in my house. I grabbed some toilet paper and headed for the kitchen. (The dining area is always called "the kitchen, regardless of its size or arrangement.) I patted my wound with the paper as I went, thinking that I could keep it clean enough no one would notice it. But when I appeared at the end of the serving line the inmate servers looked at me with open alarm. The duty guard behind the serving line raised an eyebrow, but didn't say anything. People looked up from their food at me when I entered the dining area with my tray. It was obvious that someone on the tier had seen the incident, and the word had spread. I saw where Zimmerman was sitting out of the corner of my good eye, but I didn't look at him. I sat down at the only open seat on a 4-man table and reached for a paper napkin from the pile in the middle of the table to sop up the leaking blood as I ate. Soon I had a pocket full of bloody napkins.

One of the men at the table asked me, "What happened?"

I said, "I bumped my head on the bottom of the upper bunk." That was the version that I thought I could sell.

At the top of the steps going back to the tier, after we finished eating, a guard motioned me to the side. He asked me how I got hurt. I gave him the upper bunk story. He told me to go sit down and wait on a bench at the side of the passageway.

After everyone else was locked down, the guard called me over and asked me again. I gave him the upper bunk story again. He said, "I know you don't want to say anything, but I've got to ask. And there is going to be an investigation." He motioned me over to the staff toilet and told me to look in the mirror. I went in and looked. I saw why no one was buying the upper bunk story! I had a very nasty rip alongside my left eye. It almost had a knuckle print on it!

Another guard, the one from the kitchen serving line, walked up. He held out a picture ID card. It was Zimmerman's ID. It turned out that several people had seen Zimmerman hit me and had identified him to the guard.

The guard told me, "If you didn't throw a punch, you don't go to the Hole. If you did, even in self defense, you do. What happened?"

Without being told, I knew that if I went the Hole I would lose 10 days of good time and might lose my Minimum Security status for my permanent placement, which would mean going to a hard time institution instead of a more open one. (Time would tell that there often isn't much of a difference.) My loyalty to the Convict Code dissolved. I was ready to spill my guts. A snitch is born!

Since other people had already ratted on Zimmerman, the curse was off me. I told my story, and they sent me to the infirmary to get stitched up. Stitch the snitch! Damn, a novacane needle in the forehead stings! Six stitches and I looked like Frankenstein's monster. Now, with a prison scar, I wouldn't have to get a tattoo!

They brought Zimmerman up to the infirmary to photograph his knuckles, which had lost some skin on my face. They always do that when someone gets punched out, as evidence. It turns out that it is almost impossible to hit someone in the face without leaving some abrasions on your own knuckles. Things you learn in prison that you might never have known!

I was transferred to a different tier for my "protection", one of the administrative irrationalities of prison life. Zimmerman was in the Hole and of no further threat to me. After about thirty days there, he would be sent to one of the heavy duty institutions, which he was probably headed for anyway. I never heard any follow up, but I imagine that the incident could have cost him an extra two or three years on his sentence. Crazy asshole!

And I should have thought of that when I continually mouthed off and ridiculed him. He *was* a crazy asshole, and there were a lot more like him. I should have learned a valuable lesson from the incident, but it didn't quite sink in. I had another knuckle sandwich in my future, a couple of years later.

The lesson was that the rules of verbal dispute are different in prison. Duh! In the life of an upper middle class intellectual on the streets, especially a lawyer, the goal in an argument is to logically corner the opponent, at which point you earn something in the nature of a checkmate. In the prison environment, when you logically corner someone, his first reaction is usually to resort to a defensive irrelevancy, like, "You're old!" His next reaction is to hit you in the face. Primitive perhaps, but a decisive way to end controversies.

Getting the stitches examined, and eventually removed, gave me an excuse for daily visits to the hospital for a few days, which had ended when the chemical burn on my foot healed up. I enjoyed singing while I walked through the concrete tunnel. Great acoustics! Also, a hospital visit was a chance to use a private toilet, with a seat! Small pleasures!

12

"FUCK!"

It became apparent, after I had been in prison only a few days, that the prison environment gave me an excellent opportunity to evaluate the development and usage of the work "FUCK" in the English language. Total immersion, as it were. A sentence is seldom spoken by a prison inmate that does not include the word fuck at least once. I have been in the Navy, both as an enlisted man and as an officer, and I thought that the "F" word was much used there. However, it is far more common and constant in a prison population.

"Fuck", in its various forms, is perhaps the most versatile word in the English language. In its basic form and original usage, it is a rough Anglo-Saxon word for the sex act, and is a verb: "I am going to fuck that woman!" This usage survives, but the verb form is now more commonly intended in a non-sexual, contemptuous sense: "Fuck you!" It can also be a noun: "You fuck!", or "You fucker!" It can be an adjective: "You fucking asshole!" Amazingly, it can be all three in the same sentence: "Fuck you, you fucking motherfucker!"

This is not a stretch. I heard sentences like this constantly.

Fuck can split an infinitive: "I am going to fucking break your face!" It can expand and embellish another word. The most common example is, "Unfucking-believable!"

Is this an adverb? "I can't fucking eat this meal!"

"Motherfucker" is an astonishing word. It is a linguistic staple among black men. It is both masculine and feminine, despite its maternal reference, and it can be intended both positively and negatively. Negative: "That motherfucker stole my bitch!" Positive: "She is a *fine* motherfucker!" Although it seems to lack a verb form, it is a prominent adjective: "I want out of this motherfucking jail!"

How can someone err worse than to "fuck up"? And, constantly doing so makes one a "fuckup".

It can be a ringing affirmative: "Fucking-*A*!"

13

November 8, 1998

Dear Mavis,

I'm out of stamps, but hopefully your shipment will arrive today. Otherwise my methamphetamine dealer cellie has some that he brought in with him, and I can ask him for one. Stamps are specie here, so you don't ask lightly. Guys trade them for cigarette butts, which they furtively smoke when there are no guards around. Books of matches, which are very much against the rules, seem to float around freely from cell to cell. My cellie has shifted his drug marketing skills to cigarette butts. He gets as many as six stamps for a butt, which is nearly $3.00. That makes $4.00 packs look pretty reasonable!

An armed robber in 5 House, next door, taught me how to put two pencil stubs together flat end-to-flat-end in a piece of gummed envelope to make a longer, easier-to-handle pencil. I used a Postit that came on a letter that they returned to me. I am growing more con-wise every day!

I heard the "Rodeo Song", *unedited*, on the intercom radio this morning! "It's forty below and I don't give a fuck...."

Shower and clean linen last night! Wow! I felt like a king! I don't have any shampoo yet, but I look "as good as I possibly can" under the circumstances.

Adams, the big-voiced guard in the kitchen, was at breakfast this morning:

"All right! If you don't eat Mr. Banana, don't take him upstairs with you! He's not your friend!"

Coffee cake, toast, a banana and Kellogg's Raisin Bran. Not bad. But the coffee is gross. It is a syrup, which mixes with hot water when you push a button on the front of the machine. The combined criminal minds have figured out that a new squirt of the syrup comes out each time you hit the button, so we can increase the strength of the watery coffee by hitting the button repeatedly. However, I think it is decaff. Definitely no buzz. I am told by old-timers that the coffee does not get any better anywhere in the prison system. "Five years...."

We have twenty minutes, at the most, to eat a meal. You have to prioritize and not try to eat everything. At breakfast, I give away eggs and potatoes, and often cereal, so I can have a couple cups of coffee with toast, or biscuits and jam. There is occasionally excellent coffee cake, or cinnamon rolls. I can usually get a good trade for eggs and potatoes. I have taken to asking blessing on the food on my way to the kitchen, to save time. "Lord, bless this food that I am about to eat *in a few minutes.*" I wrote to Reverend McKinney and asked him if this is theologically sound.

When our fifteen minutes are up, Adams shouts:

> "D and C Tiers, trays up! If you're through with it, bring it up! If you're not, take big bites! Don't stare at it! Bring it up! It's safe now! If you still have your corn dog, you're playing with it! Don't take Mr. Apple upstairs. He's afraid of heights! Don't take Mr. Banana upstairs. He's not your friend!"

A black guy in the cell block below me got busted last night for three pills that revealed themselves in a pat down. I don't know what they were, but an aspirin carries as much penalty here as heroin. The stupid jerk was scheduled to go to Work Camp, a minimum security, outdoors gig that cuts the length of your sentence in half if you complete the program. He will lose that, and will do hard time for a long time, as they say. Speaking of "long time", I heard one about a man who was being sentenced and asked the judge for some "latitude". The judge said, "I won't give you any latitude, but I will certainly give you longitude!"

A guard is yelling some unintelligible stuff down the tier. Yesterday morning at 6:00, he shouted,

"Christensen! Roll up your stuff! You're going downstairs after breakfast! Take it all! You're not coming back!"

I put everything together and put it on my bunk. "Everything", excluding my bedding, fit in a brown paper grocery bag. They sent some of us to testing directly from breakfast, from there to lunch, back to testing, then to the gym. No one ever mentioned the predicted move, and I ended up back in my house. I was relieved. I had been afraid that they would keep moving me one day ahead of my shower!

It got a little racially ugly last night, although it was all verbal. There are always three or four black dudes who like to "be clowning" after Lights Out at 11:00. They shout back and forth between cells, insulting each other about their "bitches". It went on until after 12:00. Loud and incessant. "Know what I'm sayin'?" There are a lot of older, steady black guys who want to sleep, but they won't interfere with the Dudes. So, about 12:30, it fell to a couple of white guys to shout, "Shut the fuck up!" That didn't go down well with the brothers, one of whom was the guy who got busted for the pills and was really wound up. There were lots of threats about what was going to happen in the Yard today., but by morning it all cooled off, and everyone loved everyone at breakfast.

You will get back my Bible, which you mailed to me. Also the postage stamps that you sent. I enclose the Offender Mail Rejection forms for each. As you can see, the mail rules are really chicken guano. We can't get books except from commercial sources, which I guess makes some sense. I have heard tell of books with pages impregnated with LSD or methamphetamines. As for the stamps, there is a limit of ten. As I said, they are used as money in commerce, and they supposedly are used for gambling debts.

I got called down to the hospital just now to have the dressing on my foot changed. I took it off and threw it away yesterday, since it doesn't look like I need it anymore, but you don't make decisions like that for yourself. Five people attended me. I felt like I was on ER!

Love, Nelson

14

MOVING DOWN THE BLOCK

My daughter's friend, Paul, told her that he had heard about "prison poetry", stuff written by convicts. So, I sent him a poem:

Poem for Paul

> Roses are red,
> Violets are blue.
> I'm here in prison;
> I wish it were you!

I was transferred from R-4 to R-1 after I got hit in the face, for my protection, according to some penal theory. I got a nice middle-aged African American cellie who was doing some probation violation time for failing to tell his supervisor that he moved out of the county. He moved from Puyallup to Kent, which are only five miles apart, but in different counties. I suspect that there was more to it than that. You have to build up a bad relationship with the authorities before they will bust you for something that small.

His general attitude toward the law was somewhat negative, because, although the principal crime for which he initially did time was violation of a no-contact order involving his ex-wife. He apparently was a major in-house marijuana grower, something he had never been busted for.

Strange, you would think, that he confessed this to me, a middle aged white guy who looks more like a prosecutor than a criminal. Just another example of the loose lips that prison inmates have in the company of their supposed peers. It is no mystery to me any more that the police can put a ringer in the cell with someone and elicit incriminating statements.

My cellie told me in great detail how to grow marijuana in a hothouse setting. The fertilization, pruning and harvesting were explained to me. Who says that you don't learn a trade in prison? In less than month, I learned how to manufacture methamphetamines and how to cultivate marijuana! There is a cornucopia of career guidance behind the prison gates!

R-1 was weird. We had mostly female prison guards. And, whereas the few women guards that we had in R-4 were women who you would readily identify on the streets as prison guards—you know the stereotype—some of these were foxes! The inmates were much more considerate to them than the animals on R-4 were to the guard dogs there. This probably had something to do with some basic man-woman motivations.

Although our security lockdown level was so high at Shelton that there was no chance whatsoever for romantic interaction between male inmates and female guards, I was surprised in my subsequent environments at some relationships that developed and were ultimately busted. I came to realize that the sophistication level between inmates and authorities is often heavily weighted in favor of the inmates. In spite of being lawbreakers, many of these guys—I have to say, particularly black men—were pretty cool dudes on the streets. Some of us were even imprisoned for crimes that involved exerting excessive influence over women. By contrast, in the rural environment of many prisons, most of the female employees are simple country girls, and they are often overweight and unattractive—easy meat for a good-looking, smooth-talking man, as in life generally. The female guards whom I knew who were exceptionally good-looking did not screw around, and had an easy power over the inmates, who generally worshipped them and kissed up to them. But, a few of the ugly ones got into relationships that cost them their jobs and got their Romeo inmate sent to another institution with a more uncomfortable lifestyle and uglier woman guards.

One of our guards in R-1 was a Russian girl, with a charming accent. She looked like Marina Oswald, the wife of the guy who supposedly shot John Kennedy. The only time we had much to do with her, or with any of the guards, was at meals or at Yard. Most of the rest of the time we were locked down in our cells and only saw the guards as they walked down the tier on their rounds.

When we were on our twice-a-day recreation breaks, which were usually inside in the gym because it was winter in Washington State, we were guarded by some casual Good Old Boys who had been in their jobs for a long time, and were well known to the many inmates who were passing through for the second, third or more times. One of the guards was a blond guy, about 35, with an enormous beer gut. He could beat *anyone* at ping-pong.

The "Gym Yard" where we were given indoor recreation breaks once or twice a day had a basketball court on one side and a volleyball court next to it. I joined in a pickup game of basketball on one of my first days, and quickly learned why Old White Guys should not try to play basketball with Young Black Guys. I saw some damn good basketball players in my time in prison. They were overwhelmingly black, but one of the best and most interesting was a Native American kid I met a couple years later who had never touched a basketball before going to prison. He was in his tenth year of a twelve-year sentence for second degree murder, and he had taken up the game in a hard-time penitentiary and spent his considerable spare time perfecting it. He could have made a small-college team.

I spent my time in the gym doing a brisk walk around the perimeter, and increasing the number of pushups that I could do. This was a tremendous physical and mental boost from the sedentary cell life of sleeping and reading.

There was also a bank of telephones on the wall, where the inmates stood in line to make calls to their loved ones. The prison telephone system is a shameless bureaucratic rip-off, which extends throughout the nation. The prison systems contract with private long distance systems, independent of legislation or oversight. All calls are collect. There is an initial connection charge of as much as $5.00 on each call, and the time is charged at more than 70 cents a minute. A five minute call from Shelton to Seattle, about seventy miles away, would cost as much as $8.00! The profits are kept by the prison bureaucracy, with no oversight or accountability, and are never reported in the Department of Corrections budget. An investigation by a Seattle television station revealed that this system produced more than $4,000,000 in one year. The system's spokesman could not say where the money went.

There was a rudimentary library in the gym. It consisted of about fifty books, mostly paperbacks, which were on shelves in the little room where an inmate porter checked out basketballs, ping pong paddles and that sort of stuff. He had a scam going with the library, telling new inmates that there was a one-cigarette price for the privilege. I didn't fall for it.

This was the beginning for me of an immense amount of reading over the next forty months. I discovered that prison libraries, generally very informal and unstructured, contain a vast and eclectic treasure of knowledge. One of the first books I checked out was "Gone Crazy & Back", a history of Rolling Stone magazine, followed by Faulkner's "The Reavers", then a history of war correspondents over the centuries. I re-read Jack Kerouac's "On the Road", which I hadn't read since to 60's. A Horatio Hornblower saga appeared, as well as a John McDonald "Travis Magee" story, always a good read, and "Passionate Sage", a biography of

President John Adams. To my astonishment, I came across a book entitled "The Fifth Continent", which was about the literary community of Joseph Conrad, Ford Maddox Ford, Henry Adams and others in a coastal town in Great Britain in the 1890's. How intellectual is that? In a casual prison library!

In the six weeks that I was at the Washington Corrections Center, where there was no organized library, my reading included, in addition to the books mentioned above:

> "The Road to Gondolfo", Ludlam
> "Grey Seas Under", Mowat
> "Ride Down the Wind", Barton
> "First Casualty", Knightly
> "The Balkan Express", Drakulic
> "Seneca", Unknown
> "Man and Superman", Shaw
> "A Time for Judas", Callaghan
> "What Makes Sammy Run" Schulberg
> "The Crucible", Miller
> "Berlin Encounter", Bunn
> "Motor City Blues", Estleman
> "The Executioner", Rolan
> "Tales of the South Pacific", Michner
> "The Gemini Contenders" Ludlam
> "A Murder of Quality", Lecarre
> "The Key to Rebecca", Follette
> "Victory", Conrad

Over the years of my imprisonment, I was to become quite a student of Joseph Conrad, finding many obscure books by him in the little prison libraries.

Time is the punishment, and time is the gift. I doubt that I would otherwise in life have had the leisure time—eons of it!—to study the entire Bible in detail. Not only did I read it from Genesis through Revelations, and many books many times; I read a great deal of biblical history and interpretations of the text. I believe that I received an informal seminary education in prison. This was part of a very healthy regimen, physical, psychological and spiritual. For a period of nearly two years, when I was in a forest work camp, I had a regular diet of nourishing, if not always delectable, meals, eight hours of sleep each night, no alcohol, six hours a week in church and twelve hours a week in the weight room. This place was probably the equal of the most expensive health spa in the world. But not much fun!

15

"CALL ME "POPS!"

My fellow inmates dubbed me "Pops" on the first day of my residence on R-4. I didn't particularly like being categorized strictly according to my age, but I *was* 58 years old, twice, and sometimes three times, the age of everyone around me. In fact, at each of the three institutions I would live in over the next forty months, I was always the oldest inmate in the camp.

I quickly learned that being called Pops was not the worst thing that could happen to me. In prison, you truly only have one chance to make a first impression, and there is little possibility of changing it. Virtually everyone acquires a nickname. You may delay the labeling by maintaining a low profile, but in the compressed life of prison, every move and characteristic is noted. Prison inmates are in constant and close contact with each other in an enforced intimacy that perhaps only Navy submariners experience. And even then, sailors get liberty and leave, so eccentricities can be deferred and eventually enjoyed in private. Prisoners are at each other's side 365 days a year, and they have little to do but watch and comment on each other. Inevitably, an inmate will get a nickname, based on appearance or behavior, which will become a part of him and will follow him from institution to institution.

There was a little flexibility in my own labeling. Over the years, I was called "Pops", "Old Timer", "Gramps", "Old School" and "O. G.", which means "Old Gangster", and is a very respectful title. Of course, you are not always called by your nickname. In my case, I was surprised to generally be called "Mr. Christensen" to my face, particularly by the black men. I do not recall any black inmate who ever addressed me by my first name, although I was often good naturedly called by one of my old-man nicknames.

An extreme example of a negative nickname came in the person of Billy Meier, a busy little guy who was always hustling food deals with stuff he pocketed in the kitchen. Billy played a lot of pinochle, and he wasn't very good at it. When he was an inmate at one of the big prisons, he ran up some unmanageable gambling debts. Normally, legal tender for gambling debts is postage stamps or purchases on store for the benefit of the obligee, since inmates have no cash. But, Billy got sudden transfer orders to another prison, and his markers were called by some criminal types, what else? He paid off the debts with blow jobs. For this, he picked up two nicknames. Thereafter, wherever he went in the prison system, he was known as "Bobbin' Billy" or "Suck 'em Silly Willy". So, Pops isn't so bad!

Most of the black guys had nicknames, which they usually brought in from the streets. Many were based on geographical origin. I had a cellie who grew up in Kansas City. He was known as "KC". Another cellie, "Oklahoma", did time in that state. There were a lot of "New York"s. One man was a cook on the streets, and was called "Skillet". Robert Nelson III was known as "Black" among his fellow African Americans. He had that name since he was a child in New Orleans. He got it because he was a shiny ebony color, remarkably black even among black people.

"Shorty" was, of course, 6'8" tall and "Tiny" weighed 350 pounds. "Dollar Bill's" given name was Bill. I don't know where the Dollar came from.

Michael Collins was a small white man with scraggly black hair, and he looked remarkably like Charles Manson. So, he was called "Charlie". I knew a couple of guys over the years called "Cave Man". They both had a Neanderthal cut to their unshaven faces, and had wild hair. The name fit them.

We had an 18 year-old Korean kid. Everyone called him "Hong Kong", which of course had nothing to do with being Korean. But, I guess Asians *do* all look alike.

16

"I'LL SEE YOU IN THE YARD!"

"The word's around that you've said some things that don't sit well with me.
You should know that words in here move like a gale across the sea.
There's a lesson that you have to learn,
And the learning's gonna be hard.
Sleep tight my friend, sweet dreams to you.
I'll see you in the Yard!

When they let us out tomorrow, to take the morning air,
My eyes will search the pavement, and I'll find your ass out there.
I've got some things to tell you, and I'll emphasize my point.
I think you'll understand, not to mouth off in this joint.

You don't have your paperwork with you, to show us why you're here.
Me and the guys on the tier think you're a child molesting queer.
You pick on little boys, and an occasional retard.
If I don't see your paperwork,
I'll see you in the Yard!

When they let us out tomorrow, to take the morning air,
My eyes will search the pavement, and I'll find your ass out there.
There's as message to be delivered, that's the custom for you creeps.
That message, once delivered, will take care of you for keeps."

Just a little tough-guy prison poetry that I composed after a couple of weeks in stir. I sent it to Paul, since he expressed an interest in that sort of thing.

17

THE SOCIAL CONTRACT

You have 500 criminals together here. All kinds: Thieves, drug dealers, burglars, wife beaters, armed robbers, murderers—the lot. We spend most of our time locked down in 2-man cells, but we are together, 50 or so at a time, at meals, and as many as 300 of us together in the Yard during recreation. Such a critical mass of felons might seem to be a prescription for a catastrophe, but a strange calm unusually prevails, often run through with an easy sense of humor.

How can this be, that hundreds of criminals, from whom society must be protected at great expense, generally get along with each other, and, individually as well as a body, with their keepers?

There are thousands of written rules governing every aspect of prison life, down to the number and type of postage stamps an inmate can have in his cell. (No "lick-em stamps from the outside. Senders can impregnate them with LSD or methamphetamines.) But it is not those rules, seldom read or given out to the population, that govern the place and keep order. Rather, it is an unwritten social contract, or, really, two social contracts that keep the lid on.

The first contract is a *vertical* one, a Rousseauian pact between the prison population and the administration, personified by the guards. If that contract has an expressible text, it was best set forth by one of the guards in a first-day orientation session:

"Act like a man and you will be treated like a man! Act like an asshole and you be treated like an asshole!"

From the prisoners' point of view, there are only a few things that they are entitled to, and that they look forward to and rely on: Food, yard time, showers, mail and Store pretty much fill out the bleak list. It is up to the administration to furnish those things as fully and as punctually as expected, and a failure to do so creates tension, since these are the things that the inmates focus on, lacking anything else in their lives to look forward to on a daily basis. Aside from that, only a general atmosphere of fair dealing and simple courtesy is expected of the guards.

However, an attitude of good humor is an enormous plus. When things are running at their very best, there is an exchange of arms-length jocularity between the population and the guards. Almost a "We're all in this together!" attitude, or, looking at it less warmly, recognition of the certainty of Mutual Assured Destruction if the contract breaks down. When things are going well, guards will laugh and respond good naturedly to remarks that might earn two weeks in the Hole in more tense circumstances.

But the veneer of prisoner contentment is thin, and easily scratched. After all, these are troubled, often violent people, who may have killed their loved ones on the outside. It takes only a minor breach of the social contract to bring ugliness to the surface.

A chicken-shit disciplinary move, like the "Brownie Incident", will always do it. After a guard fired the 9-man kitchen crew over two missing brownies (which he almost certainly ate himself), there was a sudden cold wind of hostility on the tier. Three guards, who almost never came on the tier, spent the good part of the evening talking to inmates through the bars, trying to get volunteers to replace the fired people. The kitchen is a popular gig, but there were no takers in this case. Calm was restored the next morning when the sergeant, probably not wanting to have to work the serving line himself, overrode the guard and re-hired the crew. But the inmates made a final statement by unanimously refusing to be served any of the brownies. A major sacrifice for people who see brownies very infrequently!

A major factor underlying prisoner adherence to the vertical social contract is "Good Time". When an inmate is first classified on his arrival in the system, he is given a projected release date which is two-thirds of his total sentence. If the judge sentenced him to 36 months, the release date is 24 months from arrival. One-third of the sentence is lopped off for "good behavior" and "programming". Varying lengths of time can be deleted from the good behavior award for *bad* behavior. Generally, the more violence involved in the bad behavior, the more the deduction. Anthony Cisco on our tier got into a rumble in the gym yard with a tall blond kid who is serving 19 months here, then going to California to serve a life sentence without possibility of parole. They were playing bridge at one of the stone tables in the gym. It's strange to see very bad-looking people playing bridge and chess. Here, however, bridge can be a contact sport!

The blond kid was chatting with his partner, saying things like,

"Look at those four spades playing basketball!"

Or,

"That guard over there doesn't have a heart!"

Cisco, a tough little Italian guy who in earlier, less politically correct times might have been called "a very nasty dago", took exception to the table talk. The lifer, unencumbered by considerations of Good Time, and not a devoted party to the Social Contract, brought a left hook across the table into Cisco's nose, which immediately gushed a torrent of blood form each nostril. In no time, they were up and swinging, and more blood spilled as they pounded each other against the rough concrete wall. The guards took some time getting into the fray. In accordance with standard penal doctrine, they concentrated on first neutralizing the rest of us, some 150 men who might have been incited by the action. A riot is the thing most feared in group situations, and there is an absolute zero tolerance for any activity that might start one. We were all herded to one end of the gym, while the two combatants pounded each other into bloody messes. By the time the guards, reinforced by ten more who were called by emergency radio, moved into the fight, the two men were exhausted and fairly docile. Nevertheless, they were subjected to a little Rodney King-type pummeling with night sticks and rubber hoses, and were led off with their hands cuffed behind them. The guards were not going to pass off a training session!

The blond kid was never seen again in the R Units. He most likely spent a few weeks in the Hole, then was sent off to one of the hard time institutions, in Walla Walla or at Clallam Bay. Cisco was back in the population in a couple of weeks, but he lost 30 days good time. He was punished even though he had fought essentially in self defense. If you swing in a fight, you go to the Hole and suffer the attendant penalties, whether or not you started the fight. In my case, when my smart mouth earned me a fist in the face from a fellow inmate, I was fortunate to be hit so hard that I couldn't respond. In a very real sense, Biblical injunctions of Christian behavior paid off. I didn't exactly turn the other cheek, but I let him work out on the first one. What I may have lost in macho self esteem and, perhaps, in valuation by my peers, I gained in the preservation of good time. And, in the prison environment, there is a certain respect that is gained by being in a fight and not whining about it afterward.

The second social contract in prison is a horizontal one between the inmates; not only *with* each other, but also *against* each other. It arises of necessity for the general benefit of the community, as do all social contracts, to civilize relations between the individual inmates themselves.

The basic Organic Law of the horizontal social contract is, "Do your own time and don't fuck up anyone else's." "Doing your own time" means coping with your own personal situation as best you can to maximize your chance of getting out in the condition that you desire, without blaming or relying on anyone else.

If you want to be an angel and do everything but kiss the cops' boots, that's your own business. If you want to be a total asshole and constantly push the behavior envelope, and spend your time in the Hole, that's your own business. Do your own time, but remember the second half of the social contract. Don't fuck up anyone else's time. Don't carry goody-goody behavior to the extent of snitching on other inmates. Don't be such an asshole that your behavior spills over on others and causes them to suffer your consequences with you, losing privileges or receiving punitive treatment.

Within this vague framework, convict behavior plods on from hour to hour, day to day, month to month, year to year. A commerce of mutual assistance usually prevails, born of the necessity of mutual self interest, just as among free men. New arrivals are tutored informally in important essentials, as much to keep them from clogging up the process as to help them out.

18

MOVING ON

As December, 1998 arrived, I had been in the R-Units for nearly a month. In the normal course of events, I could expect to be moved on to R-5 or R-6, which were the holding units for inmates ready to be shipped out to their "permanent" homes.

I had a session with a counselor named Armstrong, the same name as the judge who sentenced me. He looked at my paperwork and said, "Well, you're having a bad run of Armstrongs! Pretty funny. He described to me the several institutions that would suit my situation. Since my crimes were nonviolent, I would be able to go to a minimum security institution. There are five of those in Washington, scattered around the state. They are all work camps, where every inmate is assigned a job. I had heard of the Honor Farm at the Monroe Corrections Center, about twenty miles north of Seattle. It was a dairy farm. Since I come from a long line of dairy farmers in Iowa, I thought this would be a good fit. Also, it would be handy to Seattle, and I could expect regular visits from my family and friends. Armstrong checked the records and told me that there was room for me on the farm. I got the word out to everyone on the outside that we would be seeing each other soon.

Exactly one month after my arrival, on December 3, I was moved to R-5. As with all actions in prison, the move came without any notice. Several of us were told over the intercom that we should roll up our bedding and our possessions and expect to move in a half hour. The whole of my property still fit in a paper bag, so packing was not a big problem. Right on the minute, the cell door rolled open, and I carried my stuff down to the end of the tier, where I was let through to join several others who were making the move.

A guard led us through the concrete tunnel and up a flight of steps to an open alley between the buildings. We walked around the corner onto a sidewalk which ran a quarter mile across the grounds to our destination. I saw groups of inmates walking unguarded to the kitchen. I was elated. As little as it was, this was far more freedom than I had experienced in a month!

Our new digs were no classier than the old ones. The cell doors were solid, with a slit window, rather than bars, so there was a more closed-up feeling than living in a cell with bars, but the general atmosphere was much more relaxed than in our old situation. One indication of the looser attitude was the guard who made the morning announcements over the intercom. He had a distinguished British accent.

"Gentlemen! It's waffles and hot cereal at Mainline this morning! Stand by for good news about gym!
There will be *two* gyms for everyone today! One this morning, and a special Christmas program this afternoon! Yes, Christmas is coming! Have you been naughty or nice?

More news on the way! Don't touch that dial!"

The Christmas program was put on by a very good church choir. I couldn't keep my eyes dry as they sang the gospel tunes that I had sung in our church choir only a few weeks earlier. It was a nice introduction to the vast force of religious volunteers who eagerly give their time to entertain and help inmates. I was to meet many wonderful musicians from the outside in the next three years, and I was thrilled to perform with some of them in inmate programs.

We had a brief church service on Sunday afternoons, with an old white-haired preacher who could really dish it out. The service was certainly different from what I was used to. When the pastor asked for prayer requests in a normal church on the streets, people would say,

"Pray for my sister, Ruth, who is having surgery this week."

or,

"Pray for Josephine Brown, who lost her cousin yesterday."

Here in prison, it was,

"Pray for my old lady, who's on the street doing what she has to do to survive!"

or,

"Pray for my girlfriend. She's a heroin addict, and
gangrene has set in and she's going to lose her arm!"

Smoking was tacitly permitted in the rooms, which could have been a downer
for me. However, I was lucky to get a young, non-smoking black man for a cellie.
He was a very nice, clean cut guy who was serving nine months for violating a No
Contact order requiring him to stay away from a lady with whom he had been
involved. His case was typical of many that I ran into during my prison time.
Some time after the court order had been issued, he and the girl became friendly
again, as often happens, and they were together a lot. Somehow, a court official
found out, and the kid was arrested. I gave him the advice that I had given people
in his situation for years,

"It doesn't make any difference that your girlfriend fell back in love with you.
Stay away from her until the *judge* falls back in love with you and dismisses the
court order!"

In the new venue, we showered twenty men at a time in a big shower room.
This was *not* the place to drop the soap! We had a few seconds before our showers
to make our own underwear and sock selection from a pile on a table. More like
shopping at Good Will than at Nordstrom.

We walked about 200 yards to the kitchen for our meals. Again, a small taste
of relative freedom was a thrill. The food was not bad, but very institutional,
including the presentation. We had no eye contact with the servers, so it was
impossible to lobby or bargain for individual favors, which, of course, was the
purpose of the arrangement. 250 inmates at a time lined up for the food, which
came through a low pass-through, with only a hand of the server being seen. The
big room was loud and raucous, much different from the subdued little dinner
parties which we had been having in the entry units.

I was walking back from dinner one cold December night with a black man
named Veral, with whom I had formed a casual friendship. The temperature was
in the low 30's, a nasty, cold night to be out.

"I remember nights like this when I was strung out on booze and crack and
had to find somewhere outside to sleep," he said." My girlfriend had places to
stay, but on those nights she would come out to stay on the street with me."

"Gosh!", I said. "That's a great woman!"

"Yeah, she's a good woman, but she wasn't always a good woman. She's slept in the street before."

Well! Certainly another slice of life. In the coming years, I would get to know many people who had slept in doorways and under bridges on cold nights. In prison, sober and straight, they were often very pleasant, presentable men. But drugs are a great leveler.

Veron and OG were hooking me up with all sorts of people with legal questions. If I had charged for my services, I would have been rich—in postage stamps, but rich is rich! But, I never charged for legal assistance in all of my time in prison. However, I stored up a lot of good will with some very helpful people. I realized very early in my imprisonment that having friends who are large and scary looking is good life insurance.

OG was the seasoned offender whom I had met on my first day in the R-Units, and who popped up at every institution I went to in the coming years. He was like the convict in the movie, "Slam", who had an enormous inventory of popular goods in his cell, and could fix any deal. I was the new Legal Aid department in his personal COSTCO.

I was in the infirmary one last time, to have the stitches taken out of my face from my unsuccessful title defense. The nurse let me weigh myself, and I discovered that I had lost nearly twenty pounds since I checked into King County Jail a little more than a month earlier. It couldn't have been the institutional diet. I realized that the chief factor was probably the lack of alcoholic beverages. I had been sipping the beer, wine and vodka pretty substantially in my final free months. Probably over 2,000 calories a day.

Do the math! I would stay under 175 pounds throughout my imprisonment. No booze and no SOS at breakfast, and it's easy to keep your weight down!

19

THE BLUES MAN

In the transit unit we were still given two recreation periods a day, but they came with more reliability and were longer in duration than in the entrance unit. With three meals a day and two hour-long rec periods, it seemed that were *too* busy! No time to lie around the house like convicts. However, my leisure days in prison were pretty much over, except for weekends and periods later when we were locked down for several days, as in the case of an escape or other disturbance.

Rec periods were still called "Yard". We had a choice of going to the Big Yard, which was an outdoor athletic field with a track. A baseball diamond, horseshoe pits and even a couple of tennis courts. It may sound like the country club that politicians like to talk about, but none of it was country club level. Compare a Ritz Carleton to a trailer park and you get the picture.

The weather was remarkably mild for a Washington December day, and I spent a lot of time walking and running in the Big Yard. Having learned my lesson about trying to compete with younger men, I stayed out of group sports.

The other option was Gym Yard, which was an indoor gymnasium with a basketball court, one-wall handball, which the Mexicans were hot at, a couple of ping pong tables and a small weight-lifting area. There was a room, administered by an inmate, which checked out basketballs, ping pong equipment, newspapers and *guitars*! That's not a typo. Again, one should not get a picture of a posh, soft-on-convicts spa. There were two nylon-string guitars, which could be checked out in exchange for ID badges. They were old beat-in-the-ass guitars, with cracks repaired with duct tape. There were two small sound proof, glass-enclosed rooms, where the guitars could be played. One room was *always* in use by a man everyone called the Blues Man. I don't know how he did it, but when we poured into the gym, the Blues Man would already have one of the guitars and one of the rooms, and was poundin' and moanin' the blues.

The Blues Man looked as much the part as the name indicated. He might have posed for half of those pictures of ruddy old black men trudging down Alabama dirt roads with guitars slung over their backs. He was a big, solid, middle-aged man, with a Neanderthal head and a great big face that moved between emotions of great joy and deep grief as fast as his chord changes.

In the Blues Man's view, the worn guitars were "tolerable". What captures the soul of the blues better than that? "Tolerable", to one imbued with the blues, means "just fine"? When you got the blues, Baby, tolerable is as good as it gets!

He played a great blues style, using a pick that he had carved from a plastic deodorant container. They don't issue guitar picks in prison, and in the years ahead I designed many innovations for picks.

His lyrics were a mix of old stuff, his own stuff, and some combinations. Sometimes a song came out of something that had happened to him, or something he was thinking about right then. There was a lot of prison blood in his songs. One of his favorite choruses went:

> "They call me a thief.
> I ain't stole a thing!
> They call me a forger.
> I can't even write my name!
> They want me for taxes.
> I don't owe a dime!
> They say I got ten kids.
> Those little motherfuckers is all mine!"

I joined in with the Blues Man a couple of times, and I must admit that I "borrowed" this lick and put it in a song that I wrote a couple of years later, "The MCC-MSU Honor Farm Blues", which I will describe at a later point. I don't know if the Blues Man originated the lick, or if it is public domain, as most blues lyrics are. If I get rich off the song, I invite him to get in touch with me, and I will share the wealth. Of course, for all I know, he's a lifer. But, then, even a lifer needs a little walk-around!

20

THE BEST LAID PLANS...

Someone in the Department of Corrections decided that I was not going to be a dairy farmer after all. A slip of paper came under my cell door one evening. It read:

> Christensen, Nelson L. 747748
> Assigned to OCC

I read it and turned to my Cellie and asked, "What's Awwk?", which was how I thought "OCC" must be pronounced.

He said, "What's Awwk"?

"That's what I asked you!"

Jesus! Abbott and Costello as cellies!

The next morning at breakfast, I asked George the Pimp if he knew what OCC was.

> "Oh, Christ!", he cried. "That's the meanest, toughest place in the system! They work your ass off, and it's in the middle of the woods, a million miles from nowhere!
>
> You go as far as you can to the edge of America, then you turn into the forest and go another thirty miles! I was there once, and after two days I started a fight so I would get shipped out! Are they sending you out there?"

Well, George, how do you *really* feel about the place?

George drew a map of the United States on a napkin to show me where OCC was:

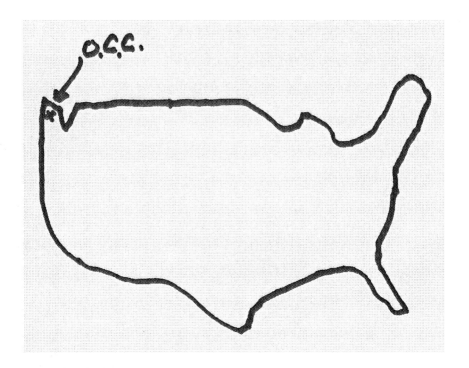

Over the day, I talked to more people about OCC and learned that it was definitely not a country club. It was a Department of Natural Resources (DNR) forest work camp, with about 350 inmates, deep in the Olympic Rain Forest at the upper tip of the Olympic Peninsula, which juts out into the Pacific Ocean on the West coast of Washington State, as far as you can go away in America. It rains all the time, except in the middle of the winter, when it snows. About half of the inmates are "DNR Rangers", who go out each morning in yellow, all-terrain buses, which they call "crummies", to thin out the forests with chain saws, build flood dikes, repair roads, and other fun chores. In the summer they are sent all over the Northwest to fight fires. The rest of the inmate population does all the things—cooking, laundry, equipment maintenance—to make the camp run. The reputation of the place in inmate folklore was that there was a chain gang work ethic, which you lived up to or you lost your minimum security classification and were sent out to a hard time institution.

My God! I was planning to be a gentleman farmer, twenty miles from home. Now, I was going to a Siberian labor camp several hundred miles of bad road from Seattle, which would mean very sparse visitation.

In looking for a silver lining to my cloud, I thought that at least I would experience a change of radio stations from the one station that was piped through the R Units, constantly replaying the hits of Celine Dionne and Melissa Manchester. As it would turn out, OCC was buried so deep in the mountains that there was virtually *no* radio reception.

I settled in for the wait for my travel orders. I was called out for a "Transfer UA", a urinalysis that is given to any inmate who is about to travel to a new institution. I never did understand the logic of this function, except perhaps as another make-work exercise for the staff. However, it is such unpleasant work that I can't imagine anyone wanting to do it. You go into a bathroom and take off *all* your clothes. The guard comes in and does a complete body cavity search to make sure you don't have a bottle of someone else's urine stuffed up your ass. Raise your arms—hold your ears forward—raise your scrotum—turn around—bend over—spread your cheeks. Then *you* put on rubber gloves, to hold *your own dick!* I can see wearing gloves to hold some else's unit, but not my own. I've been holding it with my bare hand all my life and I never got sick!

Then you get a plastic bottle and stand over the urinal do give them half a cup of urine. The guard stands there and stares at your dick while you are trying to pee under his gaze. I barely got enough out. Of course, while I was waiting outside afterward for four other guys to go through the process, I had to pee like a racehorse. If an inmate can't work up a couple of ounces of urine, he has an hour to sit and think about it. If nothing is forthcoming, the inmate gets an infraction and goes to the Hole. Since that idea scares to piss out of you, the procedure is almost always successful.

My travel luggage arrived a few nights later, a grocery store-size brown paper bag slid under the door. That would be good enough. All I had was a Bible and a few toiletries. Very few, because my Store orders had not kept up with my moves.

I could hear the guard waking up departing inmates every morning at 4. I thought of those Hemingway morning firing squads, or the condemned convict waking up to mount the gallows and return to "The green, green grass of home."

PART II
INTO THE FOREST PRIMEVAL

"Prison is good for your
health…if it doesn't kill you."

Erik Honecker, President of
East Germany, 1972

21

REVEILLE! REVEILLE! REVEILLE!

An unaccustomed softness in the black blanket of the forest night troubled my sleep and stirred up tangled dreams that I wouldn't be able to piece together later. Dreams without a message, hope or threat. Something thinned the gloomy, compressed river of darkness that poured into my window out of a hundred manless miles of dense wilderness.

A keening electric signal pierced the silent void, and the tier was instantly scoured of the night's shadows, as a single switch threw an instant, thoroughgoing fluorescence into every corner of every hallway and enclosure. The jolting electronic tone was succeeded by the Third Shift guard's call through the metallic sound system:

"REVEILLE! REVEILLE! REVEILLE!"

It was 4:45 a.m. I sat up in my bunk immediately…no snooze button here…and reached for the cutoffs that hung on the upright on the lower corner of the bed, throwing my feet over the side to feel for the rubber shower slippers which had been carelessly left out of place after a nighttime trip to the bathroom.

My cellie, KC, (for "Kansas City"), rolled awake and approximated my moves in his own practiced ritual of daily rebirth. We were both U.S. Navy veterans, and were somewhat smugly satisfied with the tidy, shipshape order which we had imposed on the little world of our prison room, in sharp contrast to the dog's breakfast of the other houses on the tier.

KC turned on CNN on his TV, while I gathered up my shower paraphernalia. He was in no hurry, as he didn't go to work until 8:00. I had to be on the job at 6:00, and go to breakfast between now and then.

For me, the baggage to the shower room down the hallway was only a lidless soap dish containing the slim remains of a bar of Dial soap, a bottle with an inch of shampoo, and a towel. When KC headed down later, he would carry a black man's toilette of powders, oils and fragrances.

No one on the tier except KC and I showered in the morning, so I had the 6-nozzle shower room to myself. There was good and bad to that. In a lifetime of living with a mother, sisters, daughters, wives and lovers, I had always run out of hot water. In my prison showers, it never ran out, but here it was *too* hot. After I would get soaped up, the leading water in the pipeline would be expended, and the scalding liquid would break through. My routine was to cope by turning on all six showers at the same time while I would go across the hall to go to the bathroom. The water temperature usually dropped to a tolerable level by the time I got back and began my shower. Of course there were no heat controls on the showers, probably due to some imagined escape threat from permitting inmates to adjust the heat of the water. Or perhaps it was because we were in a primitive forest work camp, and all facilities were somewhat crude. It was not a Best Western. Two years later, when I transferred to the Honor Farm at another prison, the showers were in private stalls, with individual controls. You cannot imagine what an enormous improvement in life that seemed to be! As I have said many times, small benefits are big things in prison.

In my time down, I learned to shave in the shower, without a mirror, using plain soap instead of shaving cream. A 23cent-per-hour wage breeds economy, and short time allowances inspire speed. I passed on a shave this day. A two-day beard is acceptable in a forest work camp with no women around except for fat, ugly corrections officers. Only discomfort caused me to shave every third or fourth day.

I was working with my sliver of Dial, which slipped from my palm like a squiggling goldfish. Safe from the legendary prison predators in my solitary shower room, I bent over without hesitation or fear to "pick up the soap" again and again. It got smaller and smaller, and eventually I couldn't get my fingernails under it to separate it from the floor. I ended up showering with my short supply of Suave Balsam & Protein Shampoo, the stuff that's $1.00 a bottle in the supermarket. It was Thursday; the day before the weekly store deliveries, so I had 24 hours and two or three showers with shampoo for soap, but that was running out as well.

No running over to the grocery store to get something when you need it.

"Store" was the sole source of toiletries, writing materials, over-the-counter medicines like aspirin, tobacco and snacks, such as candy, chips and microwave foods. The legislators who survive by telling the electoral lynch mob that inmates are living like Saudi princes had caused a ruling that we had to buy our soap, pencils and aspirin with our own money. That might not be so bad. It erects hurdles of personal responsibility far higher than many of the men had to meet in their lives on the streets. However, if it was a good thing, it was screwed up as all good things are when turned over to a bureaucracy.

Store was not a location where you could drop in to buy something when you needed it. Store wasn't a place, it was a process. Once a week, at 11:00 on Sunday night, inmate purchase forms were picked up from a suggestion box-type container in the unit.

This was the one chance to buy necessities or frivolities for the week, checking off items that were on the pre-printed form. Purchases were charged against our money accounts, which contained our meager wages and any money sent to us from the outside. Money sent in to us was charged a 20% deduction for "room and board" and other descriptions of the official theft. Store purchases were delivered to the unit on Friday afternoons. If you neglected to order something that you needed…soap, toothpaste, tobacco…you had to do without for a week or shop on a very expensive inmate black market. Some enterprising entrepreneurs made a good living in that business, particularly with tobacco. There was a King Rat on every tier, with a locker that looked like a Wal Mart. The price was usually two-for-one, and payments were made in subsequent store purchases. Store purchases were the specie for goods and gambling debts, since we were not permitted to have money. If I bought a bar of soap from King Rat on Wednesday, which went for $1.00 on Store, I would pay him back by ordering $2.00 in goods of his choice on the following Sunday night. When my Store came in the next Friday, he would be there like a mafia loan shark to collect. It was to avoid the premium price of the black market Dial that I showered with shampoo.

The cops periodically searched our lockers, and if there was an overabundance of any store items, the inmate went to the hole for a week, no questions asked or answers accepted, and his business shut down. The threat was not a deterrent.

After eight months in the camp, I had finally graduated to A Tier, "Preferred Housing", a 2-man room, with a door, which was As Good As It Gets there. The 9' by 10' cubicle was crammed with two bunks, two standing steel lockers and a small table which filled the space below a single window, looking through the perimeter security fence to the green-black wall of the Olympic rain forest. A metal waste basket and a single chair filled the space under the table. Thirty-six square feet of empty floor space remained for the necessary domestic activities of daily life. A small metal shelf bolted to the side of K.C.'s locker held his television. There was only one television set permitted to each room, and that caused some problems in a prison society drawn largely from a generation as addicted to and damaged by television as by drugs. This was particularly so when a room was shared by a black or white American and an Esponiol-only speaking Mexican alien, a common circumstance. The diversity-conscious administration furnished a couple of Spanish language channels on the TV menu. U .S. and Mexican television producers compete for new achievements in ignorance, stupidity and brain-numbing inanity. A close race, but you have to give the nod to the Mexicans. It's a shame that the officials permit the Mexicans to immerse themselves in Spanish television. Most of the poor devils, many of whom had been in the U.S. all of their adult lives, speak no more than minimal, fragmentary English. You would think that the very least they might accomplish in their time down would be the ability to communicate for necessities in their chosen country. On the other hand, what's the use? Most of them will be deported to Mexico upon completion of their prison terms. But on the *other* hand (Is that three hands?), nearly all of them will sneak back into the United States to reunite with the families that they have spawned here. One of my workmates, Ramirez, had two complete families in the U.S., one in Yakima and one in Fresno, as well as one in Mexico.

For the first four months in the camp, I lived on C Tier, known as "The Freeway". That is the Boys Town, the psychological De-Tox that is the first home for new arrivals. Two double bunks to a cubicle, without walls or doors. Four compressed, often loud men, many of whom have not shaken the crack cocaine and meth from their brain cells. Gangster rap turned up loud on boom boxes. The experience strips you of any remaining illusions of privacy. That was followed by three months on B-Tier, where people were a little more settled and mature, and men could have television sets, a negative for me. Finally, I graduated to the relative luxury of A Tier.

22

BON APPETITE!

"DNR SERVING LINE IS OPEN! DNR WORKERS ARE RELEASED FOR MAINLINE!"

It was 5:23. The cop who was just ending his night-long shift sounded the electronic tone and blasted the message indiscriminately to the eaters and sleepers, then went out to unlock the gate in the fence that was closed all night. Each of the three camps...Ho, Ozette and Clearwater...was enclosed in a cyclone fence, ten feet high, curved in at the top, without razor wire but with a fine mesh web on the inward sloping top which resisted handholds. The camps, being minimum security facilities, were open for many years, but fences were erected a few years before I got there to appease the residents of a town 28 miles away, who relied on us for employment, but feared us at night when they were at home.

As I walked toward the kitchen, a couple hundred yards away, I saw why there had been so much light coming through my window when I woke up. A blanket of snow had spread beneath a full moon in a clear sky, and the early January morning was eerily radiant. The place looked like a Christmas card!

Following twenty-five or thirty men trudging over the hill through the light snow, I thought that I could be in Siberia with Solchenitzne's Ivan Denisovich. Of course, our breakfast would be a good deal better than Ivan's!

The DNR rangers carried their black lunch buckets and their beat-up green thermos bottles. They would make up their lunches at breakfast from the selection of peanut butter and jelly, mysterious lunch meats and white Wonder Bread that was spread out on a table, and would fill their thermoses with "State Coffee", a tasteless, but very hot brew that came out of huge commercial dispensers. (My second year of Five Years of Bad Coffee.) Young appetites drove the manufacture of as many as eight sandwiches per man. There were also usually some gross-out pastries, like gigantic maple bars. We generally had some pretty good baked goods, but for a month, while the inmate baker was in the Hole, we got a steady diet of Hostess Cupcakes, Twinkies, Snowballs and Fruit Pies. More Hostess

93

products than I had eaten in the previous 55 years! On such a routine, you eventually discover that all Hostess products taste the same; they are just shaped different. And talk about unhealthy! A Hostess fruit pie has 525 calories!

Short, snug red stocking caps bobbed above heavy denim coats, which were worn and faded from repeated reissue and laundering. Under the coats were long red work shirts with "DOC" sewn in 3-inch-high letters over the left breast pocket. Inmates had to wear these either these collared red work shirts at all times, or, in warmer weather or indoors, red T-shirts. It was interesting to reflect that hunters wear red so that no one will shoot them in the woods, whereas we wore red so that someone *could!*

The entire food complex in a prison—cooking facilities, serving line, eating tables—is collectively called "the Kitchen". The serving line that we waited in this morning was backed up and motionless while the servers dished up the "Seg Trays" for the inmates who were in the Hole, the penal cells within the penal institution, to which admission was gained by breaking any one of the hundreds of rules. There were 18 men in Seg this day. I knew because part of my job as Warehouse Truck Driver and Inmate Warehouse Clerk—a six-figure title on the streets!—was to transport and act as custodian of the seg bags. A seg bag was the inmate's cotton mattress cover, into which the cops indiscriminately dumped all of his clothing and other property when he was handcuffed and marched off across the parking lot to the Hole.

About 25 of us waited in line outside the kitchen door. The snow covered the lawn 50 yards up to the Ozette Unit, where the cell windows of the Hole faced us. The lights of the slit windows switched on as an inmate pushed a cart full of seg trays up the grade of a concrete sidewalk, accompanied by a guard, as if some of us waiting in line might get impatient and steal one of the trays of lukewarm food.

Six tiny white-tail deer were gathered on the snowy grass, waiting to beg and nibble toast, pastries and apples that inmates leaving the kitchen would throw to them. Three does, each with a fawn. The fawns, which we had watched grow up since the last Spring, were nearly as large as their mothers. We seldom saw a buck, although there was a family of four which had learned to live on offerings from the back loading dock over at the Clearwater Unit. If this prison work camp is ever closed down, there are a lot of deer who will have to learn some basic animal skills.

And not only deer. The place was about as much a petting zoo as a prison. At night, a family of raccoons would sit up and beg outside my window, looking like the Beagle Boys in Walt Disney comics. Give them a Hostess cupcake and they were your friends for life, or at least until they get a better deal from another window. Nasty little devils, though, behind their comic masks. They would bite, and sometimes carried rabies, which would make them bite all the more.

Another junk food predator was the coyote. He is a sneaky, cowardly creature, who can never raise up the courage to actually come forth and beg for food. The only ones we would see were two males we named Waylon and Willie, who sat in the morning outside the perimeter security fence behind the kitchen. The kitchen workers would throw food scraps over the fence. The cowards would not move toward the food until all humans had disappeared into the building. Then they would sidle up and schlep the food away, displaying the loathing and self contempt that seems to have been installed in them by the Creator. When they would deliver the food to their pups, a sharp chorus of yelps rang out of the woods.

Crows were always with us, and among them a relatively small company of ravens. You could throw a bread crust out with not a crow in sight, and a dozen would be on it in a second. The differences between crows and ravens, which at first glance look so much alike, are surprising. The crow exhibits a raunchy, good-time air, like a happy dog. The raven, larger in body by three or four times, resembles an airborne vampire or an evil man in a black overcoat, and conveys gravity and menace. A raven takes no shit off anyone! The somber, authoritative arrival of a raven in the midst of a gathering of crows will cause an instant, unquestioning surrender of whatever food item had caused the gathering.

On such winter mornings, the kitchen line would crowd into the warm room and curl around, so that I would still be 25 people from the start of the feeding operation once I got in the door. Most of the men were quiet, as suits a 5 a.m. existence, but there were always the same two magpies, Johnson and New York, squawking in already warmed-up voices about the food which they could see on the trays of inmates already sitting at nearby tables.

> "Fucking scrambled eggs! Always fucking scrambled eggs!
> What the fuck do we have to do to get something besides motherfucking scrambled eggs?"

These guys' presence was annoying, to say the least, particularly so early in the day. Occasionally, someone would quietly threaten to kill one or both of them, and that might buy a minute or two of silence. In a prison population, a death threat is taken seriously.

The "silverware" was a mauve plastic, full-size and pretty solid. As he picked out his trio, each inmate would carefully check for food between the fork prongs and baked-on garbage on all three utensils, which was there more often than not.

When a storm caused electrical power to go out, and the camp switched automatically to generator power, the dishwashing machine, ineffective at best, would go down. Then meals would be served on paper plates, and we would get "seg utensils", Barbee Doll-size white plastic things that were used regularly to serve inmates in the Hole. It takes about a week to eat a bowl of cereal with the seg spoon. But, they were easy to smuggle back to the unit, to be applied to various uses.

Everything was full-size this morning. Just past the utensils ware stacks of plastic trays, still wet from the washer. These too deserved a careful look-over for left-over condiments and menu items that escaped washing. Likewise for the baskets of plastic glasses and cups.

The three milk spigots were barren, and someone in the line bellowed "MILK UP!", just as Alvin, a short black man with a soft, friendly face, belying his past occupation—hopefully abandoned—as a murderer, came across the room with a heavy 5-gallon plastic bag of milk in a dairy basket. The bellower, one of the mouthy ones, snarled,

> "You'd think one of those motherfuckers back there would keep an eye on the fucking milk so we wouldn't fucking run out! Isn't that your fucking job?", he asked Alvin.

The little murderer swung the milk container into the dispenser.

> "Hey, man! Fuck yourself! Don't give me any shit! We're all convicts. Give your shit to the cops!"

A good, con-wise sentiment from someone who had been down for more than ten years. Like all inmates who were nearing the end of very long terms who had served their time with good behavior, he was spending the last five years in minimum security. In the following year, I met a man who was just finishing up a 35-year sentence for Murder One.

The DNR Rangers would be in the woods all day, and they had to make their lunch at breakfast time, as well as eat breakfast. The tables were cluttered with their lunch boxes and thermos bottles. Baskets of brittle Wonder bread, which I suspected was purchased from a day-old supplier, sat beside small paper cups of butter, peanut butter and jelly. Mysterious lunch meats and varying concoctions of egg salad, chicken salad and tuna fish were dispensed with an ice cram scoop at the beginning of the serving line. Occasionally, processed cheese food slices were included, but anything remotely resembling cheese, in name even if not in substance, was usually pilfered by the kitchen crew—who were, after all, criminals—before it could make a public appearance.

The DNR Rangers were mostly young men in their 20's or late teens, with young-man appetites enhanced by long days of hard labor. Quantity, to the exclusion of any consideration of quality, was their goal in lunch preparation. Peanut butter and jelly was the combination of choice, and some men would prepare as many as eight P & B sandwiches. Two or three of these creations would be gulped down by 7:00 a.m., while the Rangers waited in their "Crummies", the yellow off-road busses that took them into the woods. It was an astonishing and revolting fact that many of these people would eat peanut butter and jelly sandwiches again for dinner in the evening. In spite of their youth and their long days of hard physical labor, many of them had the pot bellies of malnourished old men.

Not so for me! When I was first assigned to a 6:00 a.m. work shift, I was sure that my system could not get used to eating at 5:00 a.m. But generations of dairy farmers in my lineage, and the total absence of hangovers in this booze-free environment, made the adjustment easy. I had erotic dreams about breakfast during the night, and would lie awake fantasizing about pancakes and coffee.

Coffee! My Five Years of Bad Coffee continued. For a Seattle person, accustomed to a ready choice of the best brews in the world, O.C.C. was coffee Hell. I knew from my work in the warehouse that the grind was purchased from an outfit in Midland, Texas, of all places. A surprising source for coffee and Presidents. It was devoid of taste or caffeine. The first time I got hold of a cup of Folgers instant coffee, after three months of "State Coffee", the caffeine just about took off the top of my head.

Eating in an institutional environment requires self discipline and some personal rules if you are to stay healthy. This was especially so in a place where the menu was designed for loggers. Twice a week at O.C.C. they served "SOS" gravy over hash browns or biscuits. I called it "dog vomit", and not a spoonful ever passed my lips in the entire twenty months that I was held there. In fact, I *never* ate SOS gravy even once during the total forty months of my incarceration. Generally, I resolved not to eat anything that was white, or that had to be vigorously shaken off a serving utensil by the server. Not so different, it turns out, from the Atkins Diet. I couldn't see any sense in eating the Wonder bread, so I didn't. I did have a weakness for desserts. In the dessert world, I had to fall back on the "all things in moderation" philosophy.

At lunch, I always carried a couple of plastic sandwich bags that I purloined at breakfast. I was, after all, a criminal too. I surreptitiously filled the bags with raw vegetables from the bleak salad bar—radishes, cherry tomatoes, broccoli, sliced cucumbers and sliced red and green bell peppers. The red peppers were a real treat. In supermarkets on the streets they cost $2.99 a pound. I figured that the surplus was dumped on institutional markets to support the retail price. We convicts were the beneficiaries, a rare occurrence.

This collection of criminal contraband made a nice late-night snack and kept me out of more degrading foodstuffs. I shed more than 20 pounds in prison by a combination of judicious, if unexciting, eating, and no booze. Down to 165 pounds from almost 190. I calculated that my diet was down by about 5,000 calories a week from the absence of beer, wine and liquor. Not that I was a hard drinker on the streets, but, you know, that "sip, sip, sip" adds up. My work jeans were 32" in the waist, down from an uncomfortable 36". Regular time in the weight room, and crunches in my bunk, produced "Abs of Steel"!

The rock bottom of diet choice in prison is the Ramin Noodle. It is impossible to adequately describe the Ramin noodle phenomenon to someone who has not actually witnessed it. Inmates can buy a weekly supply of packaged noodles on Store, the same type of packages that are sold in supermarkets on the streets. Many men bought them by the case, and ate hardly anything else, *ever*! They lined up at the microwave in the evening, with their bowls sometimes holding as many as four packages of noodles. The noodles have a great deal of fat in them, which probably saves the eaters from starvation.

I wrote a song, "Eating Ramin Noodles Again", to the tune of "Stuck in Lodi Again". It was tremendously popular at each institution that I lived in, and when I was playing my guitar anywhere, I was asked several times a day to sing it. It became known popularly as "The Ramin Noodle Song". Once, when I was walking past the windows of the Hole at OCC, I heard the inmates inside singing it!

THE RAMIN NOODLE SONG

I walked on over to Mainline
To see what they're serving up there.
You never know what you're gonna get
When you're living on prison fare.
They had skinny, red, dried up wieners,

To serve 'em would be a sin.
But, I won't grouse, I'm back in my house,
Eating Ramin noodles again!

They say that you should never watch
Prison food being prepared.
If you see what goes in the gravy,
You're bound to come away scared.
The porter sweeps up everything,
And the cook just throws it all in.
But, I've been saved by my microwave,
I'm cooking Ramin noodles again!

I've got five different kinds of noodles,
Sitting on my locker shelf.
If anyone's gonna poison me,
I'm gonna do it to myself.
I bought double Store,
So I'd have plenty more,
And I'm not gonna share.
When I go to the Hole, I'm taking my bowl,
So I can eat Ramin noodles in there!

23

"PLEASE PASS THE BISCUITS, PAPPY!"

This was a biscuits and gravy morning. I grabbed a cup of milk before I reached the service line, and some little paper cups of margarine and jelly. It would be biscuits and jelly for me. The biscuits were consistently pretty good. "OG", my friend from the R Units, had shown up at OCC from another prison across the state, and he was the chief inmate breakfast cook. He had cooked for International House of Pancakes on the streets. You wouldn't normally think of IHOP as fine dining, but they have a lot of little tricks that dress up a breakfast. Like serving the food hot! OG brought in some of those techniques, and it really made a difference. He got the baker to throw a little buttermilk into the biscuit mix, and they came out pretty classy. Of course, "classy" on a prison scale might not make the grade on the streets. Small benefits are *so* impressive in prison.

OG stands for "Old Gangster", and is the most respectful of inmate nicknames. There is an OG in every prison population. Age alone won't earn the title. You have to have the Gangster element too. I was twelve years older than OG, so I was more "O" than him, but he was far more "G" than I was. He had a long record of violent crimes and heavy-duty drug dealing, while I was a mere white collar criminal.

OG and I were friends for almost my entire term of imprisonment, as we kept running into each other at successive institutions. We were unlikely companions, as he would appear on paper to be the stereotypical life-long black man offender, while I was an older, well educated white man who was serving time for a supposedly sophisticated scheme to defraud well-to-do people of their assets. I did some legal work on his case, and I saw his Rap Sheet, which was many pages long. Nevertheless, there were elements in each of us that did not appear evident on the surface, which drew us together. He was very bright, personable guy, who had ridden his pleasant manner through life. For my part, I was comfortable with

African Americans from my years of membership in a black church. Although, as I might discuss elsewhere, *those* black people were certainly different from *these* black people!

Incidentally, I got two years knocked off of OG's term. I discovered a sentencing error, and persuaded the Court of Appeals that the sentence was too long. This was one of my most successful cases. Overall, I calculate that I got sentence reductions for my colleagues totaling more than fifty years. Most of the relevant factors were ones that should have been discovered by their public defenders. I soon concluded that most of my "clients" had been very poorly represented by their court-appointed attorneys. Not that they had not committed the crimes with which they were charged. But, they were not represented aggressively or competently. An aggressive defense attorney can put the prosecutor at a disadvantage and negotiate a better deal for his client than a supine public defender who does not take his client's situation seriously.

The first thing I hit in the serving line was the lunch meat supply. Lunch meats were only for the DNR Rangers, but with the right relationship with a server you could get them if you wanted. Macias-Ortiz, a gold-toothed Mexican, was handing out four slices of green-tinted salami, and a single thin cut of processed cheese. I passed. He was also offering a scoop of something that could have been chicken salad or any other pulped animal. Following my, "If you can't ID the varmint, don't eat him" rule, I passed on this pate as well.

Next in the serving line, a 21-year-old black kid who seemed to spend every other week in the Hole for one unconscious minor infraction or another, was doling out greasy gravy, in which was emulsed some again unidentified body parts.

"How about some of this for the temple, Mr. Christensen?", he asked heartily.

I had established with the various members of the serving line that, "My body is a temple." They all knew that the breakfast gravies would never enter the Temple, but they enjoyed asking. Like General Patton's steward, who always offered the General a glass of orange juice at breakfast, which he always curtly refused, they never knew when I might change my mind.

I picked up a couple of biscuits, *sans* gravy. I would grease theme up with some margarine. (Talk about five years of bad coffee! How about five years of no *butter?*) I often pocketed a couple of the little paper cups of margarine to melt in the microwave back at the unit to put on my popcorn, and it tasted pretty much like butter. We had a beat-up Orville Redenbacher air popper that hardly anyone but me used, most of the inmates being happy with the micro wave stuff that tastes like suntan oil. I bought Jolly Time on store and popped it into a paper bag that I saved from a store purchase. I would dump the popped corn into a plastic waste basket bag that I swiped out of the porter's closet (Again, we *were* thieves, after all!). Then I poured the melted margarine into the bag and shook it vigorously. Add salt and shake again. Through tragic experience, I learned to let the margarine cool a bit before pouring it in, or it would melt the bag. A messy incident like that could draw the cops' attention and elicit questions like, "Where did you get the margarine?", or "How come you have a plastic bag?" With some officers, that would be enough to get you written up and set you on the slippery slope of Extra Duty and other troublesome bull shit.

I was tempted to use my red plastic DNR helmet as a popcorn bowl, but I was afraid that even though there was nor rule against it—and soldiers have used their helmets as cooking utensils, wash basins and latrines for millenniums—it might just be too outrageous for the police mentality of my keepers. I didn't want to go to the Hole for "State Issued Property; Misuse of".

Occasionally other inmates would envy me my fresh popped corn and try to use the air popper. Gomez put the margarine inside the popper, with the corn. It took me a week to clean it out.

My main breakfast course this morning would be oatmeal. Today it was served in little rectangular plastic "Seg Bowls", the disposable containers that were used to serve the occupants of the Hole. The regular solid plastic bowls had a way of disappearing into the lockers of the kitchen workers, along with the better lunch meats and nearly all of the cheese. Cheese was kept under security rivaling the gold storage in Fort Knox, but it still disappeared. Put fifty monkeys in a room with typewriters and they will eventually write Hamlet. Put fifty criminals in a kitchen, and they will figure out a way to steal the cheese.

Last in the serving line, next to the oatmeal, were the fruits and baked stuff which we were allowed to take back to the unit for snacks. Apples, oranges, cookies. Strictly speaking, according to camp rules they had to be eaten by 1 p.m. If they were found in your locker after that, they were treated as contraband, and you could get a write-up for an infraction. However, only a few cops were jerks enough to do that—the more neurotic females. It was the kind of thing that you got busted for if you were already on some cop's shit list and he or she was looking for something to get you for.

The reasoning behind the rule against saving food was that you might be accumulating it for an escape. The fact that you could keep an unlimited amount of food bought on store, which came in cans and sealed plastic containers, and could be purchased in $50 quantities, created one of those logical inconsistencies that don't trouble bureaucrats. We're talking rolls of salami, two-pound blocks of cheese, and snap-top cans of chili and beef stew. For $50.00, you could look like Woody Allen buying food for the rebels at the Deli in "Bananas"! Go figure.

The pastry issue was usually two cookies per inmate. Occasionally they would serve up a stale donut or an immense maple bar. One piece of fruit was issued as well. At best, it was an apple, orange or banana. At worst, a hard, green pear. I learned from one of the cops to put a green pear in the microwave to make it edible, but I never was a pear person.

At this end of the line there were always two cops guarding the issuance of pastry and fruit. In prison, you can always tell where the good stuff is being dished up. It has a uniformed guard standing by. A rare ice cream day, or anything with strawberries on it, is watched like the loading of a Brinks armored truck.

Plastic bags for the pastry were also handed out. They had recently limited these to two per inmate. My remark one day that we used them as condoms back at the unit was received by the guard on duty without humor.

The pastries and fruit were being handed out by Hackett, one of the regular First Shift kitchen workers. They went to work at 3 a.m. and got off duty at 11:30. It was a bitch if you roomed with one of them or lived near one in open housing. A cop would come by at 3 with his 8-battery flashlight and announce, "Jones! It's 3 o'clock!", in full public address system voice. Just another of prison's little annoyances.

Hackett was an absolutely shameless tobacco mooch. As one of the inmates said, "There's no shame in his game!" He would trade his mother for a smoke. He would hit up at least every fifth man in line with something like,

> "Hey, man! I've been giving you big servings since you came to camp. If you wanna keep it up, you gotta come up with some smokes!"

There had been a bust recently when the cops found some cigarettes hidden in the food that went up to the Hole. Four kitchen workers who worked on setting up the seg cart ended up in Hole themselves. Since Hackett was the guy who pushed the cart up the walk to the Hole, he was included among the arrestees. But when word got around about it, everyone in the camp, including the officers in the kitchen, were incredulous.

"Hackett gave someone some cigarettes? No way!"

He was released immediately by unanimous consent of his peers and his captors.

The room was filled with round tables, each seating five diners on round plastic stools attached to the tables by horizontal steel beams. The whole assembly was fixed to the floor by six bolts through a steel flange. Somewhere in the planning of the room there seems to have been a consideration that a critical mass of convicts might explode into a furniture-throwing event.

I did not have to waste my valuable time deciding where to sit. One of life's fixed certainties in prison is your eating location. In serious long-term institutions, many inmates eat three meals a day, seven days a week, fifty-two weeks a year, for fifteen or twenty years, in the same seat. Woe be to the newcomer who inadvertently sits in one of those seats!

It wasn't such a big deal at OCC, but there is always a tendency toward the Territorial Imperative in prison. One does tend to eat at the same table all the time and feel a sense of dislocation and a twinge, at least, of anger when the routine is disrupted.

Black and Oklahoma, two older black guys who had done a lot of time inside the walls, were somewhat more possessive than most. They adopted a table in the corner of the room, and Black appropriated as his own throne and lectern the seat in the very corner, facing out on the assembled diners. Black liked to "fun" and to orate in general, and this seat was his base for proving that he could "Work a Big Room."

One time a couple of Mexicans just off the chain sat at the table, and one of them took Black's throne. Black and Oklahoma raised an objection, and the Mexicans didn't back down. Rumbles in the kitchen have a zero tolerance with the cops. The four disruptants went to the Hole for "Inciting to Riot". The two Mexicans, who had just arrived that day, were shipped out to another institution. They never even had a chance to unpack their State Issue clothing.

When the cops rolled up Black, they emptied out his locker back at the unit, standard procedure whenever anyone was sent to the Hole. They discovered that, far beyond his State Issue and allowable personal effects, he had an enormous inventory of stuff from store. Black had a King Rat operation going; two-for-one advances for customers who ran out of tobacco, snacks or toiletries between store deliveries, or were impecunious due to a lack of paydays or unsuccessful gambling. He ran a Company Store that caused him to effectively own the souls of many men, such as they were in that soulless place.

Oklahoma, who was my cellie in a two-man alcove at the time, got out of the Hole in a week. I wished him no ill, but it was nice not to have to listen to his television and his big, booming voice for that period of time. Privacy is so rare in prison. Oklahoma gained twelve pounds doing nothing but sleeping and eating Seg food. For the indolent, the Hole isn't a bad life!

Black never came out of the Hole. He spent thirty days there, then refused to come out. He didn't want to go back to living on the Freeway and have to work his way back up to Preferred Housing. You lost your living privileges when you went to the Hole. For some reason Oklahoma did not suffer this fate. The refusal cost Black ten classification points, which raised him from minimum to medium custody. He was shipped off to the penitentiary at Walla Walla, a twelve-hour trip on the Chain. He was a seasoned OG, and I think that he was happier in the penitentiary scene, which, in fact, is looser and more relaxed than a DNR camp. He only had a couple of years left to do, so it was no big deal to him.

The reader might note that I constantly mention the race of inmates, which may not be politically correct. However, political correctness in racial matters does not exist in the prison environment. Race is constantly with you, and defines everything. Like all else in the compressed prison environment, race is distilled and reduced to a thick essence. And nowhere are racial concentrations more evident than in the kitchen. Walk into any prison dining area anywhere, county, state or federal, and you will see white men on one side of the room, and black men on the other, as if there were a glass wall down the middle. It's not a segregation thing, and it isn't a phenomenon that you could change with rules. It's just the way things are. I was never unwelcome across the line, and I would occasionally eat at a table with black men if I needed to talk to one of them about something. But, people like to hang out with their own kind. There is much in common among black men, in terms of humor and general culture, that a white man does not easily relate to, and the sheer volume of their group discourses can be uncomfortable, to say the least. Parenthetically, I have to say that there is nothing in the world, including a nuclear explosion, that is noisier than four black men in prison playing dominoes!

Aside from the black-white apartheid in the kitchen at OCC, two other ethnic groups had their own tables that no one else messed with. There was no threat. Their choice was just respected. The Native American Circle, comprised of Indians and wannabe Indians, had a couple tables. It was hard to say who was and who wasn't an Indian in that environment. Hell, I have some Narragansetts in my own lineage back in the 1600's, although not enough to let me fish wherever I want. Some of the Native American Circle were obviously Indians. One, for certain, wasn't. An 18-year-old Korean kid, who, in the strange assignment of nicknames, was called "Hong Kong", had been taken under the not-so-wholesome wing of one of the older Indigenous Persons, who had a well-earned reputation for absorbing young men into his web. The young Asian was a member of the Circle, which probably isn't so strange when you figure that all of the Indians came across the Arctic straits from Asia in the first place.

It seemed that some of the Indian groupies were attracted to the smoking of sage and other sacred spices at the weekend sweats that were permitted as a part of the Native American ritual.

The Asian Table was an eclectic collage of Pacific Rim cultures. It seemed that anyone with an ancestral home between San Francisco and Bangkok sat there. Japanese, Chinese, Koreans, Samoans, Pilipino, races of people who wouldn't have a polite word for each other on the streets coalesced at one table for every meal. They apparently felt that since they aren't white, Black, Mexican or Native American, they are alike. We also had a Russian and a Ukrainian who hung out together. They both spoke Russian and were too young to be tuned into Intra-Soviet rivalries.

We were allowed 20 minutes to eat our meal, whether it was breakfast, lunch or dinner. When I first came in, that seemed like a terrible rush. Eventually, I seldom took more than ten minutes, no matter how hard I tried to slow down. I told Mavis that when we went out to dinner after I got out of prison, she would have to make her reservation at 7 and mine at 8 if we are going to have dessert together. She would also have to get used to a few habits that I picked up. I would almost certainly take the salt and any leftover butter home in my pockets, for popcorn later, along with any uneaten rolls. I would try to resist bringing my plastic one-pint thermal cup, which was great for making a milkshake with ice cream and for smuggling food out. I hoped that I would be able to leave without someone shouting, "Trays up!", and to leave home for dinner without an announcement that "B Tier is released for Mainline!"

I had my own mild territorial imperative, although I was something of a nomad in that I had three different chosen seats for the three daily meals. At breakfast, I sit at a table in the main room with the serving line, my seat on the "Commodity Exchange". Trading of food items was heavy at breakfast where we shopped and bartered to fill in our individual menus for snacks throughout the workday and even into the evening. I inclined toward fresh fruits and raw vegetables, and was generally willing to part with the grosser pastries, like donuts, bear claws and maple bars, in favor of apples, oranges, bananas, carrots, celery and sliced red and green bell peppers. As I described earlier, we were allowed to keep fresh food in our lockers until 1:00 p.m., but I filled my pockets and took my stake to my job at the warehouse, then schlepped it back to the unit at the end of the workday. There was very seldom a search by the cops going into the unit after work, but they often did casual pat downs outside the kitchen when particularly portable food, like hamburgers, was served. When you saw a frisk coming, you put your contraband in the front of your pants over your genitals. No cop is going to run his hand over your cock. When they are searching us after a hotdog meal, it was fun to say, "See if you can find the weenie, Johnson!"

"Trader Mike" was in full swing this morning. A black man who will be able to make a fortune as an auctioneer on the streets, he always had at least a five-fold ration of everything by the time he got to the table, the result of collection along the way on advances and markers. The opening bid for an apple might be two cookies, but if you went around Mike directly to the younger DNR Rangers, you could reverse that and get two apples for a cookie. That pissed Trader Mike off as, he complained, it distorted the free market, which he, of course, controlled. Lunchmeats, and especially cheese slices, were the most valuable specie in purchasing fresh fruits and vegetables.

I did well this morning. I had two apples for a bedtime snack, and some celery and carrot slices, in plastic-wrap bundles to munch through the morning. With luck I'd be able to score some raw vegetables from the salad bar at lunch. In preparation, I put a couple extra plastic sandwich bags in my coat pocket.

As I walked back to the Unit, I felt like a Safeway truck. I had three oranges and two bananas in my pockets, and a peanut butter and lettuce sandwich, just in case of a late morning hunger attack. I caused a lot of puzzlement by my peanut butter sandwich formula. The peanut butter and jelly combo is a staple in prison. It seemed that no one had every thought of the peanut as a vegetable. It had always been presented to them in the form of candy, as in Reese's, so they considered it candy. When I salted my sandwich and laid lettuce on it, I drew a crowd!

24

THE BEGINNING OF ANOTHER PERFECT DAY!

I was back in my room, showered and unshaven, at 5:05 a.m. The DNR Rangers and those of us who started work at 6:00 would be released for DNR breakfast at 5:20. The 8:00 o'clock camp workers wouldn't go to breakfast until 7:30, but they couldn't stay in bed uninterrupted. All inmates had to be up for Formal Count at the Duty Station at 6:00. We would line up and pass by one of the cops at the Duty Station, and he would check us off one by one on a printed list of residents. If anyone was missing, the shit hit the fan. Early one summer morning, three inmates from our tier cut through the wire fence behind the unit, using clippers that one of them had snuck back from work. It turned out later that they had arranged for a car to pick them up on the road that ran past the camp. An escape meant a 2-3 day lockdown of those of us remaining, with very little movement outside the building. Boring! We heard that the guys were captured a couple days later at the home of one of their girlfriends in Tacoma. We, of course, never saw them again, as they were shipped to a facility with a higher level of security.

I eventually identified the racial characteristics of escapees generally. The white guys usually had more human and vehicular assets on the outside, and made arrangements (probably in person during a visitation, because our phones were tapped) to be picked up in a car by a friend, family member or lover. With the right timing, you could walk a hundred yards to the Ho Mainline Road, get into a car, and make a 2 to 3 hour run out to Highway 101 and south toward civilization before you were missed. In a couple of instances, escapees had prison jobs driving vehicles, like I did, and they just kept going. Two men in a garbage truck got to Tacoma, as did one in a run-down old station wagon full of painting equipment. I drove the camp supply truck in my job, a big white milk truck van. One day the civilian manager of the warehouse drove it to Port Angeles, eighty miles away, for servicing. A couple of the officers in charge of DNR units out in the field saw the truck going by and assumed that I was escaping. They radioed back to the camp, and things were hot for a while, even after I was found working in the warehouse. Bureaucratic momentum does not respond readily to facts.

Most of the white escapees fall victim to the limited intelligence and basic incentives that got them in prison in the first place. As soon as they can, they load up on booze and drugs and head for their girlfriend's house, and the cops are almost always waiting for them in the driveway when they get there. With luck, the escapees get a couple beers and a bit of sex before their recapture.

The Mexicans, with what I called the "Rio Grande Complex", think they are safe after they cross the first river, and are easy pickings for the cops. Often, the Mexicans turn around and try to get back into the camp by the next meal.

The black guys don't escape. They are socially comfortable and generally resigned to prison as an unexceptional element of the life style that they have chosen; at worst, a speed bump on the highway of life. They may also recognize that a black man would have to get a long way away from the camp, at least to Tacoma, 150 miles away, before he could melt into the civilian population. Beyond the boundaries of the prison camp, there were probably not more than five resident African Americans in the surrounding red neck logging country.

Sometimes when we worked all night doing the laundry of returning DNR fire crews, I would drive my truck down the highway after midnight, with a cop riding shotgun, and I was stunned at how black and forbidding the forest was, with animal eyes glowing in the trees. It would have been scary as hell to be out there on foot, dodging the pursuing search parties!

The Olympic Corrections Center was a Minimum Security facility, but it was tight. We were counted more regularly and religiously than a miser's coins. There was Formal Count at the Duty Station at 6:00 a.m. and 5:45 p.m., when we lined up and filed past the duty desk in our living units. There was Freeze Count at 10:00 a.m., 2:00 p.m., 7:30 p.m. and 10:00 p.m. During Freeze Count, every inmate had to stay where he was, whether in his room, somewhere at work, on the toilet, in the weight room or on the soccer field, for the 15 or so minutes that it took to complete the count. A PA announcement, "Five Minutes to Freeze Count!" was followed by,

"Freeze Count is now in progress!

No movement until count clears!"

Two officers would circulate through their assigned part of the camp and count the number of inmates in the area, without identifying them, and call in the number to the Duty Sergeant. If the total was even one person less than the population of the camp, some 350 people, we all had to go back to our units for At Your Bunk Count, a sort of Frozen Freeze Count. This happened with regularity in the 7:30 p.m. Freeze Count, which was during recreation time, due to the difficulty of counting groups of people such as a bunch of Mexicans on the soccer field. It came to be said that OCC meant "Officers Can't Count."

If all went well, the message was eventually broadcast,

"Count Clear!"

There was also a regular At Your Bunk Count at 4:00 p.m., just before dinner, and at 11:00 p.m., before Lights Out.

So, in total, there were seven scheduled counts each day:

Two Formal Counts at the Duty Station

Three Freeze Counts

Two Formal At Your Bunk Counts

In between all of these counts, there was an informal count every hour of the day and night, when officers would cruise their areas and mark off the inmates. Throughout the night we received hourly visits from an 8-battery flashlight.

Still, with all of this surveillance, thirteen inmates escaped in a six-month period. A disk jockey in Aberdeen, 70 miles to the South, made announcements about the "OCC Marathon". The escapees were all eventually caught, but one made it to Florida and was at large for nearly a year when he was picked up on a warrant in a routine traffic stop. We seldom ever saw the escapees again, since they were given additional sentences for the crime of escape and were sent to hard time institutions. I did, however, run into one very interesting guy a couple of years after his attempted escape. He was a Rumanian American who had been busted in a multi-million dollar computer scam, and had already done five years in California prisons. A very bright guy, whom I enjoyed quite a bit. He had a lot of resources and family on the outside, and he set up an escape plan that involved him taking off from his DNR crew in the forest and having his brother pick him up on a back road. Arrangements had been made for a flight out of the country and eventually to Rumania, where his family would join him. Rumania didn't have an extradition treaty with the U.S. Unfortunately, he got lost in the woods, missed his brother, and wandered around for a week before he was caught. I was surprised to meet him at the facility that I had transferred to after OCC. He had had 18 months tacked onto his sentence for the escape attempt, and now only had a two years to do. I told him, "Do your time, for crying out loud!" I wasn't able to follow up on him, but I imagine that he relaxed and did his time.

As I said, all of the escapees were caught. Score: Cops 13, Robbers 0. Strangely, all of the escapes took place on Mondays, which made the first day of the week pretty tense once the pattern was established. Monday became "Runday" in the vocabulary of the inmates.

Today was Monday, and Monday was Chain Day. On the first day of each week the Chain bus came up from the Washington Correction Center at Shelton with our new playmates. A normal load was 10-15 inmates. Today we would have 22, due to some special, circumstances which were not revealed to anyone in the administration here, and were probably unknown to anyone in the Department of Corrections. Inmates drift between institutions across the state in endless waves, stopping in and out of residences through a bureaucratic chaos that floods the system.

About half of the Chain arrivals would be men who were new to the system…or at least new this time…, who had been processed through he admissions center at Shelton. These guys were usually still hyper, and often still scared, having been in prison only 4 or 5 weeks. In many you can recognize the lingering effects of crack cocaine or meth, which take months to flush from their bodies. The heroin addicts were calm and quiet, thin and exhausted from weaning cold turkey from their habits in sweat-filled nights since their incarceration.

25

ANOTHER DAY AT THE OFFICE

The early morning moon had settled in the west and rested just above the sides of mountains that separated us from Highway 101 and the Pacific Ocean. Due to a phenomenon that I learned about in a psychology class in college, but don't understand, the moon is bigger and more detailed when it is near the horizon. This morning it was incredibly vivid, and the features of its landscape stood out. Someone at breakfast mentioned that it won't be this clear for 133 more years, but you know how those guys lie. We'll wait and see....

I had stopped in the DNR drying room to get a work shirt out of my locker. I was given a locker when I first arrived there because I was physically fit and, hence, Work Grade I, which meant that I could be sent out on a fire crew. Aside from the helmet and some other fire gear, I stashed extra clothing in there to make room in my regular locker for books and papers.

The drying room was kept at about 95 Degrees to dry out the DNR rain gear and boots during the night. The temperature was also favorable to rapid fermentation of alcohol-producing materials, if,—God forbid!—any should be left there. An odor of rotten apples, barely discernable over the smell of hot rubber and stale tobacco, caused me to suspect that a batch of "Pruno" was being brewed in one of the lockers.

Pruno is the generic name for any contraband booze produced by inmates. Close up some scrap fruit, sugar, bread crusts and water in a container and store it in a warm place and nature goes to work. However, quality control is very loose, and the final product is not usually subjected to a distillation process to eliminate impurities. Nevertheless, ingenuity, enhanced by the criminal mind, can do pretty well. There are some prison brew masters who crank out some almost acceptable product.

Pruno is generally a product of joint efforts in prison, because of the difficulty of gathering together the essential ingredients under the watchful eyes of the revenuers. Having a kitchen worker as a member of the group is a great advantage, due both to accessibility of food products and the suitability of kitchen spaces for the hidden brewing operation. Observation by kitchen officers is generally much looser than by the cops elsewhere in an institution, and the ingredients need not be smuggled across the grounds concealed in inmate's clothing. Also, kitchen smells help conceal telltale fermentation odors.

However, the advantage of the constant heat in the drying room is hard to pass up. To spur fermentation, it is necessary to apply heat to the mixture. That is done for you naturally in the drying room.

The members of the brewing group in one operation saved up every piece of fruit that came into their possession in a two-week period. Apples, oranges, plums and fruit cocktail. At the end of the collection phase they filled DNR thermos bottles with "Jim Jones Juice" the fruit punch of various flavors that was dispensed in a machine on the food service line, loaded with sugar. The juice was stored in a plastic garbage bag in one of the team's DNR lockers.

On brewing day, all of the amassed fruit was dumped into the garbage bag with the juice. A loaf of bread was added for yeast. The bag was filled up with water, and the concoction was sealed up with a large rubber band. The high temperature of the drying room started fermentation in a couple of days. In a closed custody environment where the inmates are kept in secure living units, the bag is sometimes placed under a running hot water faucet for a long period of time, to start the action. But here that wasn't necessary.

When the bag starts swelling, you know you have ignition. The bag is then opened daily to let out the gases which are produced by the fermentation. This is a point at which covering smells is important to prevent detection.

The product is ready for consumption after four days of fermentation. If left alone, it will get stronger and stronger, and will eventually give off alcohol fumes that can be smelled a block away, over any other odor. Timing is essential. "We will serve no Pruno before its time!"

With distillation equipment—a still—the alcohol can be separated from the impurities. However, that wasn't possible in the drying room. To purify the brew as much as possible, pinholes were punched in the bottom of the brewing bag, and the fluid was squeezed through the holes into another bag, leaving a pulpy mess behind. Of course, this was an imperfect process, and the final product was far from pure. In fact, there was plenty of still-fermenting material in solution, so the stuff would get stronger and stronger if left to its own capabilities.

This meant that an *immediate* party was called for. In this case, each of the six brewing partners took a DNR thermos of the drink to his room and nursed it in private. "Went to a party in the County Jail" is only in fiction. The prison environment, no matter how minimum the level of security, does not lend itself to keggers and cocktail parties.

Drinking alone is generally regarded as s sign of a drinking problem on the streets. In prison it is pretty much a necessity. And not only must the act itself be concealed, but the effects as well. This takes most of the fun out of the experience. As one inmate told me,

"Man, it's really scary being fucked up when everyone else is straight!"

Drinking Pruno is doubly difficult to conceal because it usually causes a wretched gastrointestinal disorder, due to its residual impurities. The last six inmates to enjoy the fruits of their brewing labors were crowding each other for toilets to stick their heads in, with nearly simultaneous reactions. And I'm not talking just *sick*. I'm talking crawl-on-your-lips, turn-your-intestines-inside-out sick!

If you want to get fucked up in prison, alcohol does have the advantage, over drugs such as pot, cocaine or heroin, of leaving the system in a few hours. A spot-check random UA will discover any of those drugs weeks or even months after their use. Alcohol can be out of the system and undetectable in as little as four hours. If booze is your abuse of choice, however, it is highly advisable to get hooked up with a reputable vodka source. Even in the isolated environment of OCC, airplane miniatures could be arranged. However, the stealth required and the consequences resulting from discovery exceeded those of buying hard drugs on the streets.

◆   ◆   ◆

I pulled a work shirt from my DNR locker and pulled it on over my red t-shirt. We were each issued four red t-shirts and three work shirts. The work shirts were also bright red, and were long sleeved, with a collar and two patch pockets. Over the left pocket, in black, 3-inch high letters, was embroidered "DOC", warning that the occupant of the shirt was the property of the Department of Corrections.

I walked past the Duty Desk and headed down A Tier to my house The bathroom at the head of the tier was full of loud men brushing their teeth and combing their unwashed hair. It seems to be a Mexican trait—if I may indulge in a racial stereotype—to clear your throat and hock out everything from your toes on up when brushing the teeth. One man, Gomez, must have once had a dentist who really got through to him with the message "Brush after every meal", and all the rest of the time too. I seldom went into the bathroom but that he was examining, picking, flossing or brushing his big white teeth, and exhaustively cleaning all of his sinus cavities. He came to the camp a few weeks after me, and whenever I moved up to a new tier I received a welcome period of respite from him, only to have him reappear one noisy morning with his movable feast of oral hygiene. I blessed the 30 days that he once went to the Hole for flunking a UA.

I usually got back from breakfast at about 5:45. I had a few minutes to stock my excess food in my locker, and maybe brush my teeth. At 6:00, the electric claxon sounded, with whatever time and rhythm the duty guard chose to play on the button. Some cops just hit it with one tone. Others seemed to think they were Van Clyburn. Following the claxon, the message blared,

> "Formal count at the duty station!
> You have 15 minutes to make count!
> Pants, shirts and ID are required!
> Don't be late for count!"

Inmates streamed down the three tiers to line up and pass by the cop at the Duty Desk. He checked each man off on a computer generated roster on his clipboard. Every cop in the camp was supposed to know every inmate's name at sight, which to me was astonishing. I've never been good at that sort of thing, and some of the Mexican names are confusing. A Mexican can choose to put his mother's maiden name after his father's, hyphenated, as a part of his surname. That yields some pretty exotic monikers.

As I filed past Officer Vo, a 25-year-old Vietnamese immigrant, he looked up at me, muttered "Christensen", and checked off my name on his list. I wondered what strange image he associated with my face to remember my name, in one of those memory systems that they teach in Cop school. "Christ-like"?

I said, "Going to work", as I always did at Morning Count, and paused for a nod or grunt of acknowledgement. I was one of only a few in-camp workers who went to work at 6 a.m. If the cops hadn't recorded my departure for work and they couldn't find me in their informal 7:00 a.m. count, I would be instantly regarded as being on Escape Status, and the shit would hit the fan. A new or unfamiliar officer might panic and start the escape bureaucracy rolling, which would gain a momentum that could be halted only after a lot of eggs were broken. To lock the system down on Escape Status, someone inevitably must be found to have done something wrong, and you can guess that it was always an inmate.

After the 6 a.m. Formal Count in the Duty Station, I walked out of the unit and left through the gate in the high wire fence that was locked throughout the night but opened at breakfast time. There was no razor wire at OCC. The fence that surrounded each of the three living units was 14 feet high, with a double layer of wire curving in for the top 3 feet.

I had a good job, the best job in the Camp as far as I was concerned. I was the Warehouse and Laundry Truck Driver and Warehouse Clerk...a very impressive title for a 23 cent-per-hour job. In addition to the minimum duties under that title, I absorbed a bunch of related responsibilities. My ability to do moving van favors for camp officials gave me a useful reservoir of power to use when I wanted to speed up the bureaucratic process when it involved something personal to me. My personal property shipments from the outside got processed much faster than anyone else's, and I could get access to medical consultation when no one else could.

My assignment as a driver was related to my being one of fewer than three inmates out of 350 with a valid driving license. The measure of responsibility and personal organization required to obtain and keep a drivers license is far beyond the levels of those qualities possessed by most of the men in prisons, a condition which is indicative of the general degree of their disassociation from society. Having a valid license says a lot more about you in that crowd than that you know how to drive.

I drove a big, square white van, just like the one that brings Wonder Bread and Hostess products in from the outer world, except that mine didn't have pictures of bread loaves or cupcakes on the side.

As I walked up the hill through the snow in the early morning, mid-winter darkness...the moon had set behind the hills in the west...my steed stood waiting, set out boldly against the dark forest behind the warehouse, a foot of snow on its flat roof. Avila and Duran, two Mexican inmates who worked in the laundry, were trudging up behind me. Off to my left, I could make out the figures of Mike Johnson, Cheeks (who was a cousin of Maurice Cheeks, the basketball player and coach, and looked just like him), and Malit, the other three of the five men who made up the laundry detachment. After months of living in this compressed environment, I could identify them and scores of other people, both inmates and staff, by their faint outlines in the dark. Familiarity breeds familiarity. The tilt of a head, the slope of a shoulder, a gait—they were fingerprints of individual identification.

Three of these men were finishing up long sentences. Malit was doing twelve years for Murder Two. Johnson was 47 years old, and he had been down most of his life. He was sent to OCC to do the last two years of his current sentence, but he was going to have to jump through a lot of hoops to get out. He was under the old Parole Board, a political patronage hangover that still governed the lives of a few dozen old cons. They would almost certainly prescribe standards of behavior for him that he would not be able to live up to, and he would be back inside, pretty much for good the next time.

You can't rehabilitate someone who was never "habilitated" in the first place. Johnson was the poster boy for that proposition. He was three-fourths American Indian. His early formative years were spent with his mother and his uncle, who were heroin addicts and users of whatever else they could get their hands on. From his first conscious thought, he was an integral part of the seamless criminal life that their habits necessitated. He was picking pockets when he was 4 years old. Not a bad age for that, when you are eye-level with the pocket! The trio traveled around the country burgling drugstores when Mike was 7 years old. The grownups would lower him by a rope through openings in the roofs, and he would rifle the store for drugs and cash. Then they would pull him back up.

"I knew Class A drugs before I knew my ABC's," Mike told me.

He said that he was such a bad kid that when he ran away they didn't put his picture on a milk carton; they put it on a Thunderbird bottle!

Mike and I had strange conversations that were like séances. We knew many of the same people in the legal world, but from different sides of the street. When I was a young lawyer representing juvenile offenders in the late 1960's, Mike was a juvenile offender in the same courts. I don't recall that we ever met, but we were side by side in the system. Juvenile Court Judge Horton Smith ruled that Mike, at 9 years old, was "incorrigible." At about that time, I mentioned to Judge Smith that I was thinking of applying for an opening as a Juvenile Court Commissioner. He told me not to do it. "It's like shoveling smoke", he said. I'm sure he was thinking of Mike.

In his late teens, Mike lived alone in a cheap motel on North Aurora Avenue in Seattle and sold drugs to high school kids. He was also a bag boy for a number of illegal gambling operations in downtown Seattle, and he carried cash protection payoffs to Seattle Police officers during that heyday of polite police corruption.

"Those were great days under Governor Rosellini", he said.

"Everyone had money!"

When he was a 9-year-old inmate in the juvenile detention facility at Fort Warden, outside Port Townsend in upper Puget Sound (an old army fort where "An Officer and a Gentleman" was filmed), Mike killed his first man. He smashed a prison guard's skull with a baseball bat. Back then, the concept of charging and trying minors as adults had not developed, so Mike's juvenile crime was washed away when he reached 18, the age of majority, and he was released. He was in and out of trouble and jail for a decade, during which time and events he developed his relationship with the Washington State Board of Parole.

The parole system was discarded in 1976, and replaced by something called "determinative sentencing." A term of confinement is set by the sentencing judge according to a printed schedule, and that's it. You do that time, less up to 1/3 for good behavior and compliance with education and work requirements. "Programming", it's called. There are no parole possibilities. Under the old parole system, the Board could release you early, but they owned your ass when you hit the streets. For any violation of the conditions of parole, the Board could throw you back in prison for a length of time up to the duration of your original sentence. The board was kept in existence to administer a diminishing number of old cons who were under that system, and, not so incidentally, to maintain some nicely paid political patronage jobs.

Many, if not most, parolees find the conditions of their parole to require of them a far higher standard of living than they were capable of meeting, and they bounce back in and out of prison. No alcohol, no drugs, constant reporting to the parole officer, stay in the county, report change of address—perhaps not impossible, but very difficult for persons undisciplined enough to have become convicts in the first place. An alcohol violation might be sufficient to throw you back in for 5 years.

Mike managed to violate his parole a bit more decisively. He killed two people. Not in provable circumstances sufficiently obvious to support formal criminal charges, but sufficiently certain to violate his parole. He had been down for nearly 14 years on that violation, and was sent to OCC to do his final three years. He was due for release soon, but the restrictions on him, even after release, would be very harsh. He would have to live in a halfway house for the first year, and he would have to stay away from the crowd that was associated with his life style, like the "winettes".

"Christensen! When we get on the streets I'll have to introduce you to some of them winettes!", Mike told me.

"What is a winette?" I asked.

"That's a lady wino!", he said.

Mike gave me crap about my $20 Timex wristwatch.

"Christensen, you can pass out and sleep all night in the gutter on First Avenue in Seattle, and you'll wake up with that watch. Those winettes only take Rolexes!"

Duran had killed several people in his life, but had never been convicted of murder. He was a very pleasant, amiable Mexican man with a wonderfully subtle sense of humor. However, he apparently did not find cheating in drug deals to be funny.

Malit, a very intelligent Filipino, had an interesting background that I never got completely unwound. He was supposedly an agent of Ferdinand Marcos in the liquidation of a number of Marcos' enemies in the Northwest US. Malit was one of the liquidators, so the story went.

◆　　　◆　　　◆

I pulled open the door into the laundry area of the warehouse. It was wonderfully toasty as the ten 75-cubic-foot gas clothes dryers have been turned on to warm them up. In a small office off the area Mr. "T" was staring at his computer screen. Mr. T was the Laundry Manager, a state civil service employee, not a cop. He was a wispy young Vietnamese immigrant with a signature Vietnamese name, Bao Truong. I nicknamed him Mr. T, and everyone but him picked up on the incongruity of the title. He assured me that he was South, not North Vietnamese, and told me how to sort out the black pajama guys who don't admit they are from the North. They can't pronounce the English "Y". It comes out "V". Maybe it's the French colonial influence. So, if "you" comes out "vu", watch out!

Mr. T handed me the keys to the truck. I walked past the dryers and the bank of commercial wash machines, into the warehouse, where my small, spare wood desk sat among lines of tall pallet racks chock full of paint cans, cases of paper towels and toilet paper, soap, generic corn flakes and rice crispies, peanut granules in 20-lb. boxes labeled "A gift of the People of the United States of America", logger boots, blue jeans, blankets, plastic garbage bags, the miserable ground coffee from Midland Texas, drywall compound, and whatever. I unloaded the snacks from my pockets and pulled a pair of knit cotton gloves from a desk drawer.

My work routine was precisely the same at the 6:00 a.m. beginning of each day. This was the 200th day of such sameness. I had to pick up the inmate laundry from each of the three units, which were three separate fenced buildings that were home to about 125 men apiece. An inmate could turn in any amount of his state-issued clothing everyday, Monday through Friday. In at 6:00, out at noon. Even Donald Trump can't get service like that these days! That was an average of three big 500-pound laundry carts per building every day. The clothing was turned in, washed, dried and returned in mesh bags that are labeled with the inmate's names. In earlier months, before the meshed bag system was instituted, the laundry was folded and tied neatly in bundles.

There was an aluminum ramp in my truck that itself weighed a couple hundred pounds. I would back the truck up to a slab in front of a unit's laundry room and slide out the ramp by hand. It ran down to the slab at about a 30-degree slope. Each living unit had an inmate laundry worker who was in charge of collecting and distributing the product. He and I lined each cart up with the ramp. I pulled and he pushed. By 7:30 a.m., I had a pretty good workout.

This morning I started up the truck, cranked up the heater and defroster to warp speed, and let it run for fifteen minutes. Better than trying to chip away a quarter inch of ice on the windshield. Still, it took me another 15 minutes to carve adequate visibility through the snow and ice that had accumulated on the truck. Then I headed slowly down the hill through virgin snow.

I was headed for Club Vega! Gilbert Vega, a Puerto Rican inmate from New York City, was the laundry man at the Ozette Unit. He had made the best of his laundry room, a long, narrow space with walls lined with numbered spaces for clean clothes. Vega had salvaged an old easy chair, or what passed for an easy chair in prison…anything softer than a wooden bench…and he always had his boom box going with jazz or blues. Charles Brown was performing at Club Vega the day before, and might be held over until today. The Sunday New York Times, which got to Vega in the Monday mail, was also on hand. When I brought back the finished laundry later in the morning, I would settle into Club Vega for twenty minutes or so, a favorite prison break in my day. Perhaps "Prison break" is a bad choice of words. Just kidding, guys!

Vega and I manhandled the laundry carts up the ramp and into the truck. This was Sheet Day for the Ozette Unit, and one of the guards, known as The Sheet Nazi, infracted any inmate who didn't turn in his sheets and pillow cases for washing on this day every week. It also happened to be once-a-month Blanket

Day, and the Sheet Nazi became The Blanket Nazi as well, so we had four carts overflowing with some 250 sheets, 125 pillow cases and 250 cotton blankets.

After loading, I backed the truck up as close to the building as I could to get a run through the snow at the short, steep hill rising up to the road. The perimeter security fence was across the road just at the top of the hill, so I had to execute a sliding right turn immediately at the top to avoid losing momentum and traction. My skills, learned and perfected in my youth on Northern Idaho winter roads, proved equal to the task.

I drove the load back to the warehouse and backed up to the loading door at the laundry room and unloaded the carts. This was easy, as the dock was level with the bed of the truck. Two similar trips to Hoh and Clearwater, and the laundry was in.

On my one-third mile trip up the highway to the Clearwater unit, I saw that Ms. Sherman, a Clearwater cop, had slid her state van into the ditch at the entrance to the camp. Women Drivers!

26

THE FIX IS IN

"Our point guard's in the fucking Hole!"

Franklin, a forty-one year old black man, was coaching the Inmate All-Star team, made up of players on basketball teams from the three camps. The inmate team was scheduled to play a team of corrections officers in two days, and Ramsey, the playground-wise prisoner point guard, had been thrown into the Hole for four days for telling one of the kitchen cops to fuck himself. The timing was suspicious, because hardly a day went by without Ramsey telling one of the officers to fuck himself, and he hadn't landed in the Hole for it up to now. Not that he didn't get a lot of Hole time, but it was always earned by a more serious infraction.

Ramsey was 26, and seven years into a 12-year sentence for crack dealing on a large and repeated scale. The long-timers like him weren't as well behaved toward the cops as the rest of us, who were always conscious of Good Time deductions for bad behavior.

Franklin knew that the fix was definitely in, but felt that he couldn't do anything about it. He asked me to use my legal skills to help. I wrote up a bunch of turgid legal bullshit, citing the Washington Administrative Code, the United States Constitution and other irrelevant authorities, and sent it up the Superintendent's office. As I had discovered in 25 years of legal practice on the streets, voluminous crap sometimes works. I suspected that the Superintendent didn't know of the artifice being practiced on behalf of the cops' basketball team, and wasn't enthusiastic about the prospect, however remote, of some legal entanglements with higher-ups. Staff legal procedures in our remote little forest camp were highly arbitrary and generally didn't respond to legal analysis, but the inmates had a leg up if a controversy threatened to go up through the system.

In any event, Ramsey walked. He didn't have time to practice with the team, but practice is not a big part of playground B-Ball. He showed for the game.

The event was set for 6:30 p.m. on Wednesday night at the gym at Clearwater camp. One hundred fifty of us from Hoh and Ozette packed into three trips on the rickety old intercamp school bus. We filed into the gym and sat on the floor around three sides of the court. No seats or bleachers for convicts! The teams had benches on the fourth side, with the scorekeeper's table between them. A very nice lighted scoreboard hung on the wall above the scorer's table, no doubt purchased from the Inmate Betterment Fund, a slush fund that we had to contribute to from our wages, and that was usually spent on items that were difficult to relate to our betterment.

The inmates were "Home" and the officers were "Visitors". Somehow, I would have felt better with the non-permanence of a "Visitor" designation. I recognized all of our players, although some of them were from the two camps other than my own Hoh camp. All were legitimate prisoners, and all were black except for one Native American, a very good player who had taken up the game during his 12-year term for Second Degree Murder. He had never touched a basketball on the streets.

All of the players on the guards' team were white. It was like an old-time Harlem Globetrotters game, with the all-black Trotters playing the all-white Washington Generals. I suspected that the cops had a few ringers, since I didn't recognize half of them, but someone told me that they drew from a couple other prison facilities in the area. However, several of them were pretty young, and they didn't have the beer gut that was standard issue for C.Os. I suspected junior college imports. They obviously had played together a lot, and they were awfully good. Very disciplined, with a tight zone defense that frustrated the hell out of the inmate homeboys. We had a little too much of the inner city action that thrives on one-on-one defense.

The game was played in two 15-minute halves. An unusual timeout was called six minutes into the second half for Freeze Count. The inmate players had to stand in their places while two officers from Clearwater counted us all. The cops' team shot lay-ups and stayed warmed up. The game resumed after a 15 minute interruption.

The referees were Mr. Pederson, who was the Rec Director, and "Black", whose real name was Robert Nelson III. Black was a 48-year-old African American who had been in prison most of his life, including 12 very nasty years at Attica in Louisiana, a prison from which it is said almost no one leaves alive. He acquired his nickname in the African American community in New Orleans as a young child because he was so black. He had been refereeing prison basketball games for some twenty years, and was as good as most NBA refs. Quick, fair and authoritative. Black called a technical foul on one of the cops for saying "fuck" while arguing a call. It was a big hit with the inmates to see a CO called for a "T" by an inmate. Strange to have the "F" word earn a sanction, when you hardly ever heard a sentence around there that didn't include it!

The cops were too good, although they almost blew it. They were as far as 16 points ahead at one time, but the inmates drew within 3 points with two minutes to go. Youth and no booze or tobacco were factors late in the game. Nevertheless, the cops held out and won, 73-68.

27

A VICIOUS KILLER

Toby Anderson, the former inmate warehouse clerk was back. He was 26 years old, serving the last 2 years of a 12-year sentence for decisively and successfully cutting a man's throat when he (Toby) was only 17. He shipped out to the Honor Farm at Monroe about a year earlier, but a recent escape up there caused an administrative panic, and they emptied the place of all inmates with violence in their records. Cutting throats apparently qualified. In the normal bureaucratic tidal shift, they would reverse the policy in a few months. In the meantime, Toby and 40 other "dangerous" people arrived at OCC on a special, unscheduled chain bus.

Toby was a nice kid. Murderers, it turns out, are generally a cut above the prison population in basic decency. We seldom saw Murder One people at OCC, except a few who were in the last five years of very long sentences, but Murder Two's were pretty common. As in Toby's case, they usually killed someone who, in an ultimate moral, if not legal, sense had it coming. Drugs and/or sexual improprieties commonly underlaid the event.

Both were involved in Toby's case. He lived in a small hick town in Southwestern Washington. The mayor of the town, a transplant from Alaska with a background of kiddie crimes, had his own Boy's Club in his home, where he furnished drugs and booze to teenagers in a tradeoff for unnatural acts. Moved by what must have been an incredibly complex jumble of psychological garbage, toned up by drugs, Toby slit His Honor's throat in his sleep. He was charged with First Degree Murder and tried as an adult. The prosecutor sought the death penalty! Newspaper articles that Toby showed me didn't suggest that any of the circumstances were regarded as extenuating. Common sense in the jury room brought the final conviction down a notch to Murder Two. Violent crimes only get 1/6 off for good behavior and programming, rather than the normal 1/3, so he would do 10 on a 12-year sentence. A long time, but he'd only be 28 when he got out. Nice to get your life of crime out of the way at a young age.

Toby and I were unloading a refer truck full of frozen beef sausage which came from one of those Midwest packing houses that you see on "Sixty Minutes". Smitty, the administrator of the food system at the camp, God love him, was a master at finding food bargains on the Internet, which perhaps gave us less-than-gourmet quality foodstuffs but enabled us to eat better than the inmates in all other prisons in the state. This beef sausage was ground up bovine products with spices added to permit it to work at breakfast, in hamburgers or in meatloaf; whatever the imagination of the cook yielded.

We were unloading the meat on a gorgeous summer day in the mountains. The warehouse stood on a hill overlooking the camp. The scene would have been perfect for a vacation "Wish you were here!" postcard. Toby was pulling pallets out of the truck with the fork lift, and I was moving them into the warehouse with a pallet jack. The driver, who had run the meat all the way from St. Louis, stood looking at the scenery while we unloaded his truck. He said to me,

"This is really a nice place! Is it for white collar criminals?"

I said, "Well, that would be me, but the guy on the fork lift is here for slitting a man's throat!"

The driver's jaw dropped, and he drifted to the other end of the loading dock, where he stayed until Toby drove the fork lift back into the warehouse for good.

28

A CHRISTMAS CAROL

Our visits took place in a wing of the kitchen. Visitors had to be on an approved list, and we could have twenty people on the list. No ex-felons. It took about a month to get approved. Since we were in such a remote location, I didn't get many visits. Strangely, visits were a little disturbing, as they were emotionally outside of the routine that I got used to.

Each visitor was searched thoroughly, and items such as cameras, knives and maps of the locale were barred. Once the visitor was cleared, we were called in the unit, and released to walk over to the kitchen. We were permitted a brief kiss when we entered and when the visit was over, but some of the guys managed to get in some pretty cozy embraces by sitting in the corners, or outside in good weather.

My friend George blew away the system. He arrived on a Saturday a few minutes before visiting hours were over. I saw him for five minutes before he had to leave. He promised to come back on time the next day, Sunday. On Sunday I waited for my visit. Two of the three allotted hours went by. Finally I got my call and walked over for the visit. George was sitting at one of the tables. He told me that he had camped the night before, and his van was stuck in mud when he woke up. He had to get a tow, which explained the delay. He pulled out a map to show me where he had been. A *map*! How in hell had he got a map through the search?

"George! Put that thing away! How did you get that in?"

It turned out that he had chatted up the guard the day before, and formed such a good relationship that the guard did not search him when he returned on Sunday. That was very unusual.

As we talked, I saw George cleaning his nails with a Swiss Army knife. A *knife*! What else did he have on him? It turned out that he also had a camera, which I warned him to keep in his pocket. Jesus! I could go to the Hole for the rest of my life!

At the end of every visit, inmates were subjected to the indignity of a strip search. A guard watched as I took off all my cloths, and then he put me through the standard routine, including,

"Bend over!"

"Spread your cheeks!"

At the end of this visit, and every visit, I was taken into a small room and put through the routine. I said to Peterson, a nice young guard,

"We have to stop meeting like this"

He replied,

"I'll always have the pictures!"

◆   ◆   ◆

My youngest daughter, Erica, who lived in New York City and was a producer at VH-1, came to visit twice over the holidays. A nice effort, much appreciated, to come from the Eastern extreme of the nation to the very Western.

As with everything that the women in my family do, the visits turned out to be legendary events. When any of my three children, Erica—-25, Jean—-30, or Nelson, Jr.-35, came home for visits, their mother, my ex-wife, Vangie, liked to spend as much time as possible with them . On this occasion, when Erica drove up to see me, Vangie rode along as a passenger. She and I were on good terms generally, but she was not on my Approved Visitors List, which permitted only 20 names, and I did not expect to be visited by her. When my other daughter, Jean, came up, she and Vangie booked in at the Forks Motel, 30 miles away, and Vangie waited there while Jean visited me. For this visit, Erica and Vangie signed up at the Forks motel.

Erica showed up a half hour too early for the beginning of visiting hours at 10 a.m. I saw my little red truck driving toward the exit and wondered what the hell was going on. The cops won't let anyone sit in the parking lot, so she had to go explore the Rain Forest for a while. Seeing my truck for the first time in a year was like getting a glimpse of an old lover.

Erica came back and we had a nice visit. When she left, she picked her mother up from the Forks Motel and they made a lucky ferryboat connection from Port Townsend to Whidbey Island and got back to Bellingham by early evening.

Erica promised to come to see me again on Christmas day, but I didn't intend to hold her to it. I knew that she would be spending Christmas Eve with Vangie's family, about 2 ½ hours south of OCC, so I was accessible. However, I had no idea what she would do with Vangie if she came to see me. I had given strict instructions against anyone coming to the camp and trying to bluff through the system.

The beginning of visiting hours at 10 a.m. Christmas morning came and went, and I settled into a normal weekend routine of reading, writing and dozing. It didn't look like I was going to have a visit, a result that I was resigned to. At about 11 a.m., the P.A. sounded: "Christensen to the Duty Desk!

The message for a visit would have normally concluded, "…for a visit!". When I got there, Officer Potter handed me the telephone, which *never* happens. I took it.

"This is Inmate Christensen."

"Christensen, this is Sgt. Hall. How do you feel about your ex-wife?"

Instinctively, I almost said, "How much time do you have?" I caught myself. Hall was the duty sergeant in charge of the camp on the Christmas Holiday.

"I have no problem with her, why?", I said, the familiar realization creeping over me, not for the first time in my life by any means, that the women in my clan had created another unique crisis.

> "She came in with your daughter, and she's not on your approved visitor's list. You can visit your daughter, but I'll have to call the lieutenant at home about the other one."

I checked out at the Duty Desk and walked the 200 yards to the Kitchen where visits took place. Erica was there, her face flushed and her eyes red from tears. I knew that she had tried her crying act, which is usually capable of breaching any security barrier. It hadn't yet worked this time, but knowing these women, I knew that the game wasn't over.

The officers had told Erica that she could come in but Vangie couldn't. No one is permitted to wait in vehicles on the property, so Erica drove her mother a half-mile up the road, left her there to read a book in the pickup, and walked back toward the entrance to the camp.

One of the guards was driving down the road from Clearwater camp, a third of a mile away. He must have blinked his eyes when he saw a well-dressed young blond lady walking along here in the forest 30 miles from the nearest town or residence. He gave her a ride to the Kitchen and heard her tearful version of the story. Another addition to my camp notoriety.

After Erica and I had talked for a few minutes, one of the officers, came over to our table and said, "We're going to let her in."

A half hour later I looked out the window and saw the top of my little red pickup gliding through the parking lot beyond a line of cars, then swing smoothly around the end of the line and into a space. Amazing! Vangie was blind as a bat from glaucoma, with about 20% vision at best. She didn't have a license and hadn't driven in years. At least if she was committing a crime, she was in the right place!

She got out of the truck and came through the visitor's entrance. Having broken every bureaucratic rule in letting her in, the cops didn't even bother to process her, which involves taking a Polaroid picture and opening a file. Her face, like Erica's, was red and swollen from crying, but she came by it honestly. She had gone through an unsettling hour or so. She had been reading a book down the road where Erica had left her in the truck. She looked up and saw three uniformed officers approaching. Visions of Randy Weaver and David Koresh must have flashed through her mind.

All's well that end well. We had a nice visit and added a new chapter to the bizarre Christensen history.

29

FELIZ NAVIDAD!

This winter wonderland a few days before Christmas had a good feel to it. My spirits were pretty good on this, my third Holiday season in prison, compared to the first year, when I had only been down a couple months. Then in self pity, I wrote a poem and sent it with my Christmas cards to my family and friends:

"I WON'T BE HOME FOR CHRISTMAS"

I've gotta get through what I've gotta get through,
I've got things and time to do.
And you can't know how I'm missing you,
But I won't be home for Christmas.

I've got Christmas cards and colored lights in the yard,
And a lot of little things.
They're supposed to help, but they make it hard,
And I won't be home for Christmas.

I know there will be many other years,
And I hope we spend them together.
But that's an awfully long time from now,
Through a lot of stormy weather.

So have a party and trim the tree,
And raise one to my health.
But don't set a place at the table for me,
'Cause I won't be home for Christmas.

Maudlin!

This year my message was more upbeat:

"OCC CHRISTMAS RAP"

T'was the night before Christmas,
And all through the tier,
It's the inmate consensus
Saint Nick won't come here.
The closest we'll come to warm Christmas arms,
Is a two-pound box from Hickory Farms.

My cellie just hung up his one Christmas card,
There are lights on the duty desk and out in the yard.
But I felt down on my luck and pretty depressed,
'Cause Christmas in prison isn't the best.

Then on the back dock there arose such a fuss,
I thought it must be the Clearwater bus.
I made my way out through the cigarette smoke,
To see if the noise was some kind of joke.

What I saw made me think I was out of my head!
There was a crummy, painted a bright shiny red!
The door swung open, and without a pause,
Down the steps came Santa Clause.

Santa at OCC was a duck out of water.
Beneath his beard he looked like Officer Potter.
He stood right there in the middle of the dock,
And handed out pardons signed by Governor Locke!
Then he brought out the champagne and popped all the corks,
And shouted, "Jump in!,
The party's in Forks!"

Being so far out in the wilderness, we didn't get a lot of off-campus Christmas entertainment coming in, but there were a few nice people who made the trip. A combined choir from churches in the area put on a very good Christmas concert, and the Christian Motorcycle Association brought in some guitar music. They were a fun bunch. They didn't ride their bikes on their winter visit, but they came up a couple times in the summer, and they brought about 100 classy motorcycles, which the inmates enjoyed looking at in the Chapel parking lot. A micro-nice version of Sturgis.

Christmas breakfast featured pancakes, link sausages and two fried eggs. Plenty of hot coffee, marking the end of my second year of "Bad Coffee". Not bad. Overall, we ate well, especially on holidays. Christmas dinner! What a spread! We had a big, thick slice of ham, turkey, yams, corn, peas, salad, pineapple slices on the ham, eggnog and four kinds of pie! With linen table clothes! A very nice meal, with lots of heart in it. God love the kitchen staff!

Even greater than the Christmas dinner was the feast at the chapel, a week earlier. A number of the church volunteers from Forks annually brought in buffet dinner that would have been suitable at a Four Seasons hotel. Maybe that's a prison exaggeration, but you get the point. Hot dishes of good country food. Salads and desserts! A crowd of 150 devout inmate Christians, who never visited the chapel on any other occasion, packed the place. Unfortunately, all manners were forsaken, and men at the front of the line piled their plates with such abandon that they threatened the happiness of those behind them. However, the volunteers had done this before, and they brought more than enough food. The guards had also done this before, and we were patted down as we left, to ensure that we didn't schlep any food back to the units. But *we* had done this before too, so our accumulated criminal expertise got more food through the pat down than Sherman marching to the sea.

Not everything was as positive. We rode the bus over to the chapel at Clearwater for a Christmas Eve program, and it was cancelled because the people putting it on were afraid to drive on the snow-covered roads.

"The birth of Christ has been cancelled due to inclement weather! Ozette gym is open!"

By Christmas morning we had lost our White Christmas to the rain. "I'm dreaming of a slushy Christmas". It doesn't work. To add to our cheer, it was announced that the telephones would be out, at least for the day. Hence, no Christmas calls to our loved ones. That bummer was handled with typically ironic prison humor and further typically cynical rumors on causation of the outage. The prevalent conspiracy theory was that the inability to call out of the camp created an "Emergency Situation", which entitled the guards to double-time pay.

Not the greatest Christmas, but not the worst.

30

A DEATH IN THE PRISON FAMILY

The Clearwater bus that transported inmates back and forth from the Clearwater camp was chugging up the hill from the highway, fishtailing a bit on the snow that had been compacted by several trips that the bus had already made that morning, as well as by the cars of officers who came and went at the 6 a.m. shift change. The bus moved confidently without chains, as the daytime driver was Townsend, an inmate from Eastern Washington who was familiar with snow driving. Townsend was a farm boy who had driven trucks since before he was big enough to see over the dashboard. It was a pleasure to ride on his bus and feel the fluid grace with which he sang through the gears. The night time driver, Rapu, was half Sicilian and half Apache, with a resulting temperament that was reflected in a driving style totally different from Townsend's. Ragu crashed through the gears, and his bus jerked down the highway and often stalled from climbing the hill in 5th gear.

The Clearwater unit was three tenths of a mile down the Hoh Mainline, a private paved logging road, from the rest of the Camp. Also over there were the DNR shops, the chapel, the infirmary, the School, such as it was, and the principal Rec Center, with a gym, a weight room and one racket ball court. The Law Library was over there too, but it didn't have very many books, and the typewriter was always out of commission. Law Library of the Damned. Whenever an inmate found anything there that was of use in his battle with the administration or the courts, the book soon disappeared.

All inmate movement between Clearwater and the rest of the Camp was on the Clearwater Bus, except special transportation by van, and except for work vehicles, such as my warehouse truck. The bus was an ancient yellow school bus that was purchased years earlier for $400.00. It was quite literally and visibly held together by gray tape and wire, mostly old electrical cords.

All of the Clearwater inmates rode the bus at least three times a day for meals at the main camp. The guys on our side rode it over there at night for gate, if we wanted to use that rec center instead of the smaller one at Ozette, or to go to a religious event at the Chapel. When the bus picked up inmates at the Hoh and Ozette, the officer on board counted the passengers and radioed the message "70 out from Hoh (or Ozette) with 40", "70" being the bus cop's radio ID number; "40" the number of inmates aboard.

The Clearwater inmates were a surly looking lot on their regular meal runs, staring vacantly out the windows as they rolled past. The trips were one more annoyance in a life full of annoyances. The night time rec loads were, by contrast, a jovial mass of Convicts at Play. I was reminded of the difference between week-day subway passengers in New York City and the trains on weekend nights, packed with happy revelers with a few pops in them.

On this trip, the bus was full of inmates going to a memorial service for Fausto, a 56-year-old inmate who died a few days earlier. He was the driver of the camp garbage truck and had a stroke while behind the wheel. Of course, the suc-ceeding medical care was as primitive as you would expect in a remote forest camp without a MD. The circumstances were somewhat mysterious as well. Fausto was apparently punched out by his cellie in their two-man room the pre-ceding weekend. The cellie was pissed off because he was trying to sleep, and Fausto was slamming his locker door. The issue had apparently come up before. Lopez, a neighboring roomer, broke the fight up, and on the basis of their analy-sis of the facts, the cops took the cellie and Lopez to the Hole. The cellie was going to be charged with assault; now it might be murder of some degree, although causation would be hard to connect. In the long run, the cellie was not charged with *anything*, after the bureaucracy screwed up the investigation.

The Chaplain had come to see me while I was inventorying some clothing in the warehouse. My blood froze when I saw him, because there are not many good circumstances under which a chaplain comes to see you. I was afraid that some-one in my family had died. Or perhaps that my sentence had been modified, and I was to be led off to the gallows, to return to the "green, green grass of home"! It turned out that he wanted to ask me to sing "How Great Thou Art" at Fausto's memorial.

Fausto was a big man. Not fat; big and strong, with a large head and a fear-some mustache. He was Mexican, of the outgoing, jovial type. Everyone knew him.

About a hundred men rode the bus over to the chapel for the memorial ser-vice, in two loads. Fausto's family was there. Three brothers, his widow and his son. One of the brothers, who looked like Fausto's identical twin, without a mustache, was in a wheel chair, as was the son. I never found out why. The camp superintendent was there, as well as some other officials.

Sometimes an event is overwhelming not just on its own merits, but because it is so incongruous with its setting. I seldom saw more than thirty people in the chapel at one time, so this was quite an impressive gathering. Over a hundred convicted criminals. A little church packed to the walls with burglars, drug dealers, forgers, swindlers, thieves, and murderers, on a wintry Rain Forest day. An unusual scene even for these elements, but except for the red institutional shirts and padded denim convict coats, you wouldn't have been able to figure out where these people came from.

Pastor Morlen led the service. He was a gentle, quiet man in his 50's. His intense Christianity was clothed in a softness that made you take him lightly at first. His depth revealed itself as experience with him increased. He hadn't organized the program, other than to ask me to sing. Men went to him to volunteer, and the result was amazing, particularly for a spontaneous gathering of convicts a million miles from nowhere. "Black" (Robert Nelson III, a black inmate) sang "We're Gonna Walk Around Heaven." Two Mexican men read scriptures in Spanish, and Valentine Martinez played the guitar and sang a sad Mexican song. Pastor Morlen read a poem by KC ("Kansas City"), who couldn't get off work for the service, and three men from the Native American Circle sang a ceremonial Indian song to a somber drum accompaniment, and presented the family with a sacred talisman that they had prepared. I cut "How Great Thou Art" to two verses, because it seemed awfully long for the occasion.

Four races paying their respects in a deeply heartfelt way, drawn from a population of hardened Enemies of Society.

The "twin" brother wheeled to the front and thanked everyone. We went through a line and shook hands with the family members. The mother had to hold up the hand of the little boy in the wheel chair so we could shake his hand. There was coffee and punch afterward, and assorted pastries that looked familiar. Pastor Morlen took unspoken advantage of the delayed electric clock, that hadn't been reset after the morning's power outage, to avoid the one-hour limit on the service.

PART III

ON THE CHAIN AGAIN

"YOU DON'T KNOW WHAT LONESOME IS
'TILL YOU'VE STARTED HERDING COWS."

Cowboy song

31

A CHANGE OF SCENERY

The regulations required a minimum stay of twenty months at Olympic Corrections Center before an inmate could get a transfer to another, less remote, camp. I had originally expected to do my time at the Honor Farm at Monroe Correction Center, a prison dairy farm twenty miles from Seattle, and as soon as I could I applied for a transfer to that facility. I didn't know too much about the place, but I had learned a few relevant facts. Number one, it was less than a half hour drive from Seattle, so I could expect more visits than I had been getting in the forest. Two men who had been shipped back to OCC after an escape occurred at the Honor Farm told me that it was a much looser place, with less invasive searches and much lighter discipline. That didn't mean too much to me, as I could deal with the searches and discipline at OCC. In fact, I was comfortable with the tight OCC discipline, because it produced an orderly, predictable atmosphere. Nevertheless, I looked forward to a somewhat relaxed time in my final year of confinement.

In anticipation of my move, I wrote a song, to the tune of Willie Nelson's "On the Road Again":

ON THE CHAIN AGAIN

"On the chain again.
I just can't wait get on the chain again.
Going somewhere else to see old convict friends
I just can't wait to get on the chain again.

On the chain again.
Shackled up to my traveling friend,

141

We're wearing orange so people know where we've been.
I just can't wait to get on the chain again.

CHORUS

On the chain again!
With Every mile my new home's getting nearer.
On the chain again!
With OCC in my rear view mirror!

On the chain again.
I just can't wait to get on the chain again.
Going somewhere else to see old convict friends.
I just can't wait to get on the chain again."

I sang the song along with my other standards at the Ozette rec center where my guitar was kept, and it quickly became a camp favorite, along with "I Want to be a DNR Ranger" and "The Ramin Noodle Song".

Playing the guitar at the Ozette rec center, which was the only place where I had access to it—other than at the chapel—was quite an experience. The place consisted of a weight room, a game room, with table tennis, pool tables and a foos ball table, a gymnasium and a so-called music room. The music room was almost always used for meetings, and I seldom was able to get in there. I nearly always had to play standing in the hallway just outside the gym. The acoustics were vibrant, and the noise from volleyball games or basketball games made it literally impossible for me to hear myself.

Nevertheless, I usually drew an audience. Someone would always bring up a new inmate to listen to some of my favorites. I got very tired of singing The Ramin Noodle Song, but it stayed at the top of the charts.

One of the advantages I would find in my new home at the Honor Farm was that I could keep my guitar in my room, when I eventually got a room. With all the dead time on hand, I got a lot of valuable practice in a few months.

In mid-July, my boss at the OCC warehouse called me in and told me that I would be leaving on July 30. I was stoked! The downside was that I would have to go back to the Washington Correction Center at Shelton, where I had started my imprisonment a couple of years earlier, to stay for a week until the chain left for the Honor Farm. Going back to close confinement in a maximum security prison was not appealing. However, I was a hardened, proud inmate by then, and every hardship and indignity rolled off my back. I was ready for anything that came my way as a part of the price of getting back near civilization.

The day came. The chain bus rolled in with it's cargo of new OCC inmates, and the officers chained us up for the ride. It was later than most chain departures, since the bus had come on a three-hour trip from Shelton. Nevertheless, we were on board by 8:00 a.m., and headed on the thirty mile ride to Highway 101, then a hundred miles to Shelton. The same Highway 101 that goes south to the Mexican border starts near Forks, Washington. The sights along the way on our southward journey were exciting to me. After two years of looking at nothing but trees and wild animals, *everything* was exciting to me. I remember that there was an automobile dealership across the road from my new home at Monroe, with one of those annoying loudspeakers on which the phone operator pages the salesmen all day. I *loved* the sound! It was a reentry to civilized society.

We rolled down the highway in good humor. Everyone was glad to be heading for the renewal of a new location. Hardly anything ever changes in prison life, so anything new is an exciting event.

When we arrived at the Washington Correction Center, we went through the same admissions routine that we had been subjected to when we first entered the system, except that we already had ID badges and shoes. On this trip, they let us keep our shoes. Another difference was our swagger. We knew the ropes, and the cops knew that we knew the ropes. It was almost like we were on the same side, us against the world.

We walked across the grounds to the building that held people who were waiting for transportation to a new facility. Thank God we didn't have to go to the entry units, which are really tight. When we got to the building, I was told to pick up a mattress off a pile and top take it to my cell. I knew then that I was going to be the "Rug", the third man in a two-man cell, who would have to live and sleep on the floor due to overcrowding of the prison. Being the Rug is about the most unpleasant thing that a person can experience. You take up almost all of the floor space in an already unpleasant room, forcing the other inmates to stay in their bunks all of the time, except when they go to the bathroom, which is also a very unpleasant experience, since you are lying right next to the toilet

I was only the Rug for three days, which seemed like a lifetime. Eventually, one of the other two guys moved on, and I was left to the considerable comfort of being one of only two men in a two-man cell.

The food was really lousy compared to the meals we got at OCC. There were also none of the advantages of relationships that I had built up in the OCC kitchen, which had guaranteed special treatment from the guys on the service line. Due to my job as the supply truck driver and my legal services to many inmates at OCC, I had become something of a potentate in the kitchen. It wasn't the best food in the world, but I got it as good as it got.

This was a week to sleep and do nothing. It was strange to not have a job to do. At OCC, we all had jobs and were expected to work hard at them. I stayed in my bunk and read and slept the dead time away. At meals and in the rec breaks, I met a lot of inmates who had crossed my path in the preceding two years. They were always different than I remembered them. The forces of a prison location forge an inmate's personality, and when he gets into a new location his personality changes.

On the Monday following the Monday of my arrival a week earlier, I was "On the Chain Again", headed north to the Monroe Corrections Center, just twenty miles past Seattle. It was awesome to see familiar sights. We actually passed within a mile of my home! I felt a strange rebirth at being near familiar things.

I had seen the Monroe Corrections Center many times over the years, but only from the highway. It sits on a hill just outside the town of Monroe, Washington. The portion of it that is visible is a frightening rock structure of a classic old prison design, with guard towers at the corners. As we drove up the hill in the bus, I could see that there was a lot more to the place than the big old prison structure. We first pulled into a complex of more modern building, where a few of the passengers were herded out and turned over to the resident guards. Some of the guys who had been to Monroe before passed the word that this was the Sexual Deviant section, which caused us to give new looks to the guys who got out. However, you couldn't be sure if the new arrivals were sex criminals, because prison crowding necessitated that some regular prisoners be placed there, which is a frightening thought. I later met some normal young men who had lived there for several months; handsome guys who you would think would be at jeopardy. They told me that they hadn't known whether to sleeps on the stomachs or their backs!

It turns out, however, that sex criminals are kept so drugged up that they are generally pretty harmless in the population. As we drove out of the complex, we went by a garden area where about fifty inmates were working. They looked like zombies as they drifted slowly and dreamily around the space. Months later, an inmate barber told me that when he was taken over there to cut hair he had to strap his customers in the chair so they wouldn't fall out.

But the drugging didn't always work. They story went around that one sex offender managed to get something sharp in his cell and he cut off his nuts and handed them through the bars to a guard. Ouch!

You hear a lot about prison rapes. There were a few gay inmates everywhere I lived in prison, and some you would have to call predators, always on the lookout for "fresh meat". My observation over the years was that gay people got together voluntarily, just like on the streets, and vulnerable men who got taken advantage of were people who would have been taken advantage of on the streets. Violent rape is rare. I met a couple of guys who told me that they had been raped in another institution, but their stories reminded me of man/woman cases that I had been involved in as a lawyer years earlier, in which a sexual encounter became rape when it was discovered and publicized, to the embarrassment of the "victim".

Our chain bus wound through the grounds. Eventually it stopped in front of a large gate in the rock wall of the old prison that looked like a medieval draw bridge. After a wait of about half an hour, typical for government action, the gate moved upward and the bus entered. My God! We were going inside the maximum security prison! I was supposed to be going to Minimum Security. If there had been a mistake in my paperwork, it might take weeks to straighten it out.

It turned out that we were only taken inside the walls for processing. I learned later that nearly every special function, such as serious medical treatment, was inside the walls. The Minimum Security facility was only a satellite to the Big House. We shuffled off the bus, chained two-by-two, and headed into a long, high-ceilinged room. By this time, I was a very smooth customer in chains and had no trouble moving along with my less-experienced partner, who was coming straight from the county jail to begin his sentence. I was an Old Gangster!

There was a big cage with a bench around the inside. We were "dechained". We sat down and waited. Eventually, we were called by name, one by one, and put through the paperwork of prison entry. When we had all been processed, we filed out informally, with supervision by only one guard, and were led across an expense of driveway to a gate in a cyclone fence. We were now regarded as Part of the Family. The guard unlocked the padlock on the gate, and we entered the world of minimum security. We stood uphill from a complex that looked like a 1950's grade school, with a neat lawn and clean one-story buildings. Only the coils of razor wire on top of the fence surrounding the buildings suggested that this was not a place to educate 8-year-olds. But, that's not a bad thought then you think about 8 year-olds.

This was a loose place, compared to my most recent long-term home. Inmates strolled around the grounds. There was a large recreation area with a baseball diamond and backstop. Several men were jogging on the rutted, uneven track that surrounded the baseball field. Signs warned the inmates to stay six feet away from the fence. The armed guards in the towers of the Big House gave effect to the warning. As we strolled to the property room to draw our bedding and clothing, we saw inmates passing casually in and out of a library building. We could hear the sounds of a volleyball game come from a gym.

"This is going to be a hoot!", I thought. Not so fast....

32

DOWN ON THE FARM

So, here I was, Down on the Farm. However, I hadn't seen the farm, and I didn't even know where it was. I certainly couldn't see any cows where I was. That would change before long. Cows and I would become very close.

Because I was a new inmate at this facility, I had to start at the bottom of the list for housing, which meant that I was back in an open dorm. It would take me about six months to get into a two-man room. In the meantime, I had to live the crowded, noisy life of a dorm resident, with a bunch that often included some really fucked-up people. I had to get my cranky old man demeanor back on, which I had found out to be the best defense against fucked-up people. This was a definite step back from the comfortable quarters that I had worked my way up to at OCC. But, nothing good ever lasts in prison.

A supervisor came by and asked for volunteers for kitchen work. I had never worked in a prison kitchen, but I knew from observation that it was pretty good duty, as long as you didn't get stuck with a nighttime shift. I volunteered, and I soon found myself helping to prepare dinner and cleaning tables during and after the meal, and scrubbing the floor after the meal. Meal preparation did not include much actual cooking. Most of every meal was prepared inside the main prison, and trucked down in thermal containers. We just had to break it down and serve it on plastic trays. There was no interaction with the customers, as the trays came to a window on a roller line, already loaded. We did have to set up the salad bar from scratch. Don't think Four Seasons Hotel salad bar. Think Greyhound Bus Station salad bar.

One of the nice things about kitchen duty is that you are working for civilian food professionals, not cops. In this case, the head of the operation was Alice, a nice country lady about my age. She appreciated good work, and I gave it. She rewarded us with ice cream and other special treats. Of course, we would have stolen them if she hadn't given them to us. After all, we were criminals.

The job was the softest job I ever had in my life. I showed up for about two hours for dinner prep. Then I had two hours off and returned to work the dinner and cleanup after dinner. The empty time was my own! I went to the library and read the newspapers. The Seattle Times! The New York Time! The Wall Street Journal! Died and gone to Heaven!

All too good to last. After a couple weeks of kitchen duty, the cop who was in charge of staffing the Farm showed up with a press gang. He came right into our work area when Alice wasn't there, and marched us off to an introductory lecture about the Farm. I guess this had been his modus operende for some time, and Alice didn't have the clout to fight it.

The next morning at 7:00, I was in the Mud Room, which was the dressing room for Farm workers. Through a window in a wire cage, we were issued ragged blue jeans. We had drawn work shirts as a part of our general property issue, thin gray long-sleeve collared shirts. Since it was still summer, we didn't get coats, but when the weather turned cold, we would get thinly padded denim jackets which were essentially worthless for keeping you warm.

We changed into our work clothes and went through a door to the gymnasium next door. There, we milled around with all of the other inmates who were going to jobs outside the fence. About sixty of us were going to the Farm. The rest, another fifty or so, were mechanics, fire fighters, groundskeepers, etc. When the Farm workers were called by name from individual cards held by a cop, we went through the door. Outside, we were patted down for contraband. I could never figure out what they were looking for in this search. What do you smuggle *out* of a prison? After the search, we again loitered until we were called for the Farm Bus, a blue and white converted school bus that chugged diesel fumes outside of the fence. When the gate was opened, we walked to the bus. There were always some assholes who ran to get a favored seat. There was absolutely no standard on which to grade the seats, favorable or un.

There were a few passengers who were not Farm workers. We stopped to let them off at their jobs, and then headed down the hill to the highway. We turned right at the bottom of the hill, and headed through the town of Monroe. The Bus had a loud radio, which by general consent was usually tuned to Howard Stern. In this demographic sample, Howard's grossest antics were appreciated as the highest possible culture.

The drive down the main street of Monroe was both refreshing and painful. On the one hand, it was wonderful to see people going about the normal life that we would eventually re-enter, going in and out of coffee shops, and on our return trip at the end of the work day, taverns. But it hurt to see a life so near and yet so unreachable.

We left the town on a highway headed south. The Farm is four miles from the prison. After we traveled about two miles south, the bus turned right and the Farm was only a couple hundred yards farther. The bus pulled into a gravel driveway. The driver, who was a corrections officer, had a deck of cards with our names and pictures, and he called the roll. We got out when our names were called. We lined up and were patted down again, as if someone had run alongside the bus and handed drugs or weapons through the windows.

This was the year 2000. The Farm had been established in 1905 and operated continuously ever since. It was a dairy farm, milking about seven hundred cows. They were Holsteins, which are milked three times a day. The milk was delivered to prison facilities, jails and state hospitals throughout the state of Washington. There were three shifts of farm workers, including a graveyard shift that ran from midnight to 6:00 am. Although that seemed like a terrible gig, there were people who liked it. A prime benefit was that you got immediate assignment to a two-man room when you started working the shift, in spite of your position on the housing list.

The conditions in which the cows lived would break your heart. Contented Cows they were not. They spent their idle hours, when they were not being milked, in an enormous open-sided barn with a corrugated metal roof, in which thousands of pigeons roosted, stealing the grain which we fed to the cows. We were to have some interesting battles with the pigeons, which we eventually won through methods which would not get a trophy from the Society for the Prevention of Cruelty to Animals. Of course, the society wouldn't have cared about the pigeons once they saw how the cows were treated.

There were six big pens, in which the cows were separated according to their stage of calf bearing. The cows which were very pregnant were in a seventh pen, right next to the milking parlor. There was no bull. The veterinarian had an almost full-time practice artificially inseminating the population. He would let us try it if we wanted, inserting our arms up to the shoulder into the cow's uterus, with the tube of sperm alongside a rubber glove. I did it once, and I got a reaction from the cow which was about as good as I ever got from a woman. Of course,...Oh, enough of that.

There was a lunch room in the admin building where we checked in for any special announcements that were to be made. One of the inmates was the porter, in charge of cleaning and stocking the building, including the lunch room. One of his duties was to keep a big coffee pot going. The coffee was typically bad prison coffee (My third year of bad coffee), but in the winter it was nice to have it. You could stick your head in there anytime for a fill up.

For most of the time I worked on the Farm, the porter was Chris Avery, a 30-ish guy who was an aspiring film writer, and I don't doubt that he did well after his release. He was a walking tabloid, and knew absolutely *everything* about all public figures. I had always wondered what the "distinguishing feature" was that Jennifer Flowers identified on President Clinton's dick. I asked Chris if he knew. He did. "Dogleg left", he told me.

The cows lived on concrete covered lightly by straw. They never saw open fields or grass in any form. There lives were an endless circle of walks a quarter mile to the milking parlor on a concrete pathway and three milkings a day. They were an unhealthy lot, with constantly sore hooves and ankles, which further enriched the vet.

We had to get rubber boots from a disorganized supply which reminded me of the slipper selection in the King County Jail on the second day of my imprisonment. Boots were scattered randomly around a couple of filthy dressing rooms. It helped to have friends, because inmates hid good ones in their size against a need in the future. As I have said before, the possessory drive is strong among prison inmates.

There was no way that you could go around the Farm without some sort of boots, since you were constantly walking in cow shit, sometimes a foot deep. In August, it was not too bad, as the ground and cow shit dried up. In the winter, good boots were critical.

I found a pair of boots which were too small and had a hole in one of them. I figured I would work with that and keep a constant eye out for an improvement. I came up with a nearly new pair within a week, the product of a trade for several sack lunches, which I generally didn't care for. More Mystery Meat and little tear-up packages of mustard and mayo.

There were three classifications for the inmates who actually worked with the cows. The "milkers" were in the in the milking parlor. They applied the milking machines to the cows' teats and were the people who actually produced the milk. Their job was extremely hard work. The toughest people I knew at the Farm were milkers.

The rest of us, responsible for getting the cows to the milkers, were "herders" and "pushers". The herder was the real cowboy, but they didn't give him a horse or a six gun.

I was made a herder right off on the first day. Instead of carrying a six shooter, I carried a rake. The cows were milked in a set order, according to their color designations: green, black, red, yellow, white and blue, represented by colored chains around their necks. I would open the gate to the green pen and a few of the approximately 125 cows in there would get up and stroll out of the pen, taking the turn toward the door which headed for the milking parlor. Most of the rest I had to shout at or hit in the rump with the rake to get them to go. As I got more experienced, I could get them going without violence or much noise. I learned that approaching them from a certain direction would do, or using certain words. The Cow Whisperer! But cows are very, very dumb. And they weigh about 1,500 pounds. You were warned and quickly learned not to let them get you between them and a solid object, like a steel fence. They could, without any evil intentions, crush your ribs.

I directed the herd along a quarter mile paved path about 15 feet wide and bounded by a wooden rail fence on each side. Not exactly the Chisholm Trail. There were a couple of turns, and the stupid beasts tended to stop and jam up at the corners, as if they didn't know where to go on a route that they had traveled hundreds of times. I would have to push my way through the herd of packed animals to get up to the front and encourage the stalled cows to move along. But, after unclogging them, I had to get back to the rear, because there would always be stragglers if you weren't back there. If a cow was particularly difficult and slow, I would sometimes pick her out and make her run back to the barn after she was milked.

I was not Gene Autry, but I was a cowpoke nonetheless. And moreover, a *singing* cowboy!

I would herd my cows to the gate of the pen in front of the milking parlor and wait for the pen to empty out. Then I would open the gate and muscle my animals into the pen, and close the gate behind them. Ten cows at a time went into each of the two sides of the parlor, and it was the job of the pusher to get them in there. That was no mean fete. Here again, although the cows had done this three times a day for years, the stupid beasts often didn't remember the routine. Also, something might have spooked some of them, which made them unmanageable. I usually help the pusher with my cows, because it was a very tough job until you had a lot of experience. After several months, I could make them do my bidding fairly easily.

When the ten cows in a group had been milked, it was my job to get them out of the milking parlor, down the two alleyways that ran outside of the lanes in which they had entered the parlor. This was not too difficult to get started, as the cows knew somewhat instinctively that they were headed back to their stalls, which, as unpleasant as they were, did have feed and a thin bed of straw to lie down on. However, once out of the building, they tended to bunch up, so I had to slap some cow butt to get them moving. I seldom ventured into the alleyway, as it was very narrow, with concrete walls, and provided an opportunity for bone-crushing squeezes between cow and wall that I had learned to avoid. This area also contained a danger that I had not foreseen.

33

GUNFIGHT AT THE OK CORAL

I usually sat on the top rail of the holding coral outside the milking parlor while I waited for my herd to be milked, unless the pusher needed help. Some of them didn't want any help, as they had their own system with the animals and didn't want their rapport disturbed. One pusher, a farm boy from Eastern Washington, had somehow developed a pet/master relationship with one of the 750 cows. The beast followed him around and nuzzled his neck with her big wet nose. This was strange, since cows are generally totally unemotional.

One day in the late fall I was sitting on the rail while my "green" herd was being milked. Fashad, a Pakistani inmate was the pusher. Fashad had acquired the not totally illogical nickname of "Camel", and that was what everyone called him. Camel was doing time for fraud. He had been in business as a landscaper, and he had been convicted of taking large retainers from homeowners, then never showing up to do the job. It surprised me that this would be a crime. I thought that all landscapers, painters, roofers and their ilk did that all the time!

Parenthetically, Camel was released from prison shortly after I was. Not much later, I read in the newspaper that he had been deported, as most immigrant criminals are, was returned to Pakistan, somehow made his way back into the U.S., and was again charged with the being a crooked landscaper. Talk about recidivism! Poor Camel will do a lot of years this time around.

Anyway, Camel was not a very good pusher. He waived his arms and shouted at the cows, which only scared them and froze them in their place. This day they were not getting into the milking parlor fast enough, and the milkers were running out of cows to milk, which was about the worst thing that could happen on the Farm. Dan Johnson, one of the milkers, a cocaine dealer with a very nasty attitude, jumped out of the milking trough and ran out into the pen, shouting obscenities.

"Can't you fucking do your job, Camel?"

He looked at me, sitting on the rail.

"You fucking lazy ass! Why don't you fucking get down and help him"?

Now, part of the whole web of survival in prison is that you don't let other inmates insult you publicly. As cool and sophisticated as you might be, you have to slip back into street ethics a bit, or the unanswered insult will get around the facility and be talked about, and you will lose face in the community. Perhaps that's illogical, but prison society is not based on logic.

I stayed on the fence and replied,

"Don't call me names, punk!."

Well, another rule is that you *never* call another inmate a punk. The "P Word" can not be received without retaliation.

Johnson ran across the pen and lunged at me. I swung back off the fence and avoided his blow. He was beet red, and was screaming at me. But his milking partner was yelling at him to get back on the job. He gave me one more acidic look and disappeared into the parlor.

I figured the incident was over, and gave it no further thought. About a half hour later I went into the exit lane to move my cows out. As I turned around at the end of the lane, I caught a glimpse of an unusual movement out of the corner of my eye, and WHAP!!, I took Johnson's fist in the mouth. My hat fell into a river of cow shit. Johnson jumped back into the milking trough, shouting, "Motherfucker!" over his shoulder.

In line with normal prison inmate logic, my first thought was to make sure the cops didn't see my injury. If they did, I would be hauled back to camp and would get involved in the whole investigative rigmarole. If Johnson was punished, and he certainly would be if the cops found out, I would be regarded as a snitch and would lose face in the complex inmate social structure.

However, the security aura on the Farm was a lot different than in the tense high-security facility where I had been punched out the first time. On the Farm, we worked for civilian dairy farmers, who didn't care who did what to whom, as long as the job got done and they themselves didn't catch any shit. There was only one cop on each shift, and he came around once an hour to count us. I got a Band-aid for my lip in the wash shed, and told anyone who asked that I had been kicked by a cow, not an unusual event, although they didn't usually kick that high. Nevertheless, everyone in the area knew what had happened. Although Camel hadn't seen me get hit, he saw Johnson's earlier actions, and he saw me come out of the milking parlor bleeding from the mouth. The story got into the inmate communication network, and by the time we were back at camp at the end of the day, everyone knew that "The Old Man" had been punched out.

I think I said sometime earlier in this narrative that one of the best things you can have in prison is large black friends. I had a bunch, and they were pissed off when they heard what had happened. One of them, Big Ben, was the inmate pastor in our Protestant congregation. He weighed over 300 pounds and was a scary looking guy, but, as fit his religious role, he was a real sweetheart. However, if you weren't an acolyte you wouldn't have known his good side.

Ben motioned me over to his table at dinner that night. He looked at my bruised lip and knew that it had not been injured by a kick from a cow. There was no use persisting in the cow story with him, but I told him that I probably deserved it and I didn't want there to be any retaliation. Ben said, "We're going to talk to him."

That evening, Ben and another very large black inmate cornered Johnson in the rec building and dragged him into a remote bathroom. Ben told me later that they "'splained" things to him and never let him lose the impression that he was about to die, until they let him go.

Johnson steered clear of me in the in the prison camp and at the Farm. However, a year later we both went to work release at the same facility in Seattle, Bishop Lewis House, where only about 40 men lived. We struck up a casual nod-of-the-head relationship and had no tension. But one night when Mavis picked me up to go to dinner, she almost drove over him in a dark crosswalk a block down the hill from Bishop Lewis. The next day he spoke his first words to me. "You sure carry a grudge!", he said. "You had your chick try to kill me!"

34

MOVIN' ON UP

After about six months of herding cows in sunshine, rain, sleet and snow, I had an opportunity to politic my way into an indoor job in the dairy office. I kissed a lot of ass and took advantage of subtle racism among the civilian farm personnel. They preferred to share office space with a white man, if only because African American inmates tend to be pretty loud. Racism isn't so bad if you are in the right race!

I was put in charge of receiving and processing the dairy orders from the Farm's customers around the state of Washington, about seventy public facilities, mostly prisons, county jails, and state mental hospitals. We sent out our trucks every night to deliver to the customers in the morning.

It was a pretty slick operation, but my function was very low tech. I could not initiate phone calls, and my computer was not connected to the Internet, so I could not send or receive e-mails. All of the orders came in by telephone. My isolation was due to the fact that fertile criminal minds in my position had in the past devised ways to abuse the communications system to their personal advantage. The Department of Corrections response to any abuse by one inmate was to deny access to the abused system to all of the thousands of other inmates.

The Farm had been established in 1910 and had operated continuously for ninety years. It was a dream business. It owned the land and had no mortgage obligation on it. It had no debt service other than 30-day obligations for current purchases of supplies and equipment. Being a government entity, it paid no income or other taxes. It had a captive...literally...customer base, and sold milk products to them at prices set by the federal government. It had virtually no payroll for its employees. Our starting wage was 35 cents an hour and we worked up to a maximum of 90 cents.

Nevertheless, that Farm was losing money, and the decision was made to sell the cows and close the business!

In my office position, I had access to the financial statements for the operation. Everything appeared to be in the black until you got to the administrative costs of the involvement of officials from the state headquarters. The bureaucrats couldn't keep their hands off of a cash cow, and they drained the profits and shifted unrelated costs to the Farm. The result was a net loss.

You always hear about government waste and incompetence, but it usually seems hard to believe. My employment on the inside gave me a valuable lesson in just how bad things really are.

The state sold the herd of 750 cows to a dairy in Pendleton, Oregon that produced milk for some cheese factories. We loaded them aboard a convoy of trucks one day, and ninety years of farm operation ended. The sale brought a half million dollars. I'm sure that didn't show up in any accounting records shown to the legislature.

The sale took place six weeks before I was scheduled to be sent to Work Release. Since I didn't have a job during that period, I got in a lot of guitar practice and lot of legal work for inmates. My "three hots and a cot" continued.

I used the time to write a song:

MCC-MSU HONOR FARM BLUES

"Well, they brought me here on a big white bus in chains.
Yes, the brought me here on a big white bus in chains.
They make me push cows in the wind and the snow and the rain.

I wonder if my baby ever thinks of me.
I gotta wonder if that woman ever gives a thought to me.
She needs a full-time man and I know I can't be free.

> They charged me with robbery;
> I never took a thing.

> They charged me with forgery;
> I can't even write my name.

> They charged me with taxes;
> I don't owe a dime.

They say I got 12 kids;
Those little buggers is all mine!

I got the MCC-MSU Honor Farm Blues.
I know I can't win; I know I got to lose."

I fell in with some other musicians and we had a good time playing loud
music in a tiny room in the rec center. We worked up some arrangements of my
various prison songs for an upcoming in-house concert on Labor Day. I named it
"The Mud Room Concert", because the performers would stand on the concrete
slab in the back of the Mud Room, where we dressed and undressed before and
after hour shifts at the Farm. The slab overlooked the baseball field and track.
The audience, truly a "captive audience", sat on the ground looking up at the
show.

I sang "I want to be a DNR Ranger", "The Ramin Noodle Song", and
"MCC-MSU Honor Farm Blues", all my own compositions, as well as Merle
Haggard's "Mamma Tried" and John Cash's "Folsom Prison Blues". I got the
same cheer that Johnny Cash did when I sang, "I shot a man in Reno, just to
watch him die". I was a hit!

The next day a surly young guy came up to me and said,

"You were pretty good yesterday. I thought it would suck, but it wasn't that
bad."

I've had worse reviews!

35

RELIGION IN STIR

"Alyoshka looked at the sun and rejoiced. A smile
came to his lips. His cheeks were sunken, he lived
only on his ration and didn't earn anything extra.
What was he so pleased about? On Sundays he
spent all the time whispering with the other Baptists.
The camp didn't worry them—it was like water off
a duck's back."

One Day in the Life of Ivan Denisovich

Alexander
Solzhenitsyn

Jailhouse conversions get a bad rap on the streets, and by normal standards
that is probably justified. Prison inmates seldom carry their commitment for long
after they are released. However, the beneficial effects of religion in prison, Protestant Christianity in my own experience, cannot be overstated.

Every prison in the State of Washington has an official chaplain on its staff. At
OCC the chaplain was Art Morlin, an Assembly of God minister from the small
neighboring town of Forks. At MCC-MSU, in Monroe, Washington, where I
worked on the dairy farm, the Chaplain was Sister Patricia, a Roman Catholic
nun. The chaplains supervised the practice of a host of religions, most of which
had little to do with their own faith. Their supervision of these other faiths was
administrative, not spiritual.

Religious practice included not only main-line Protestant and Catholic Christians, but Jehovah's Witnesses, Muslims, Jews, Native Americans and Wickens.
Prison administrators recognize the stabilizing effect of religious practice, making
their own jobs easier. In addition, there have been court decisions protecting the
religious rights of prisoners.

A Catholic priest would make weekly visits to hold mass. The Jehovah's Witness preachers came in weekly with their black briefcases. (What's in those things?). The Muslims, mostly black men, handled their own meetings and seemed to have a prayer routine that did not include all of the prayer events of standard Middle East Islam. The Indians had a lot of feathers, pipes and other paraphernalia in their meetings. They had permission to go on all-day sweats in specially constructed huts on Saturdays, where they could smoke some non-narcotic herbs. They were subjected to urinalyses when they came back.

Many people associate the Wicken religion with witchcraft, which is not correct. It is a Norse religion, with Thor and a bunch of those other guys. I was once told that it is the leading religion in Iceland. It is a "man's" religion, and was popular with the lumberjack crowd at OCC.

My own experience was with the Protestant operation. Because we had Pastor Morlin at OCC as a full-time chaplain, we were very active. I attended some type of religious meeting three evenings a week, and was part of a service that was held for inmates and their guests on Sunday morning. As I said earlier, six hours a week in church and twelve hours in the weight room produces a very healthy person.

A great benefit of our church relationship was being able to meet with volunteers who came in from the outside to worship with us, entertain us with music, bring us snacks and to generally provide us with some decent and sane people to talk to. The Christian Motorcyclists were an amazing group of people who came all the way up to the woods at OCC with as many as fifty classy motorcycles that the inmates drooled over. Some of them were musicians, and they entertained us, which was very rare in our remote location.

I noticed in my prison years that the Protestant church attendance was generally about one-third of the inmate population. At OCC, we had very few black members, although the camp population was about 50-50 black and white. At MCC-MSU, which was close to the cities, and where many African American ministers and musicians came in from the streets, our church membership was over 50% black. Regardless of racial makeup, the songs were the same and the Scripture verses were the same.

I don't want to be a Bible pounder, but I have to give credit where credit is due. Attitude is more than half the battle in prison. Depression and anger are easy to come by in the prison environment. I used to say that when you go to church you "meets a better class of people", to quote the old joke. Hanging out for several hours a week with men who are focused on something other than the day-to-day grind of prison life, and see a bigger picture beyond the petty crap that surrounds you all the time, is a huge attitude elevator. If you can get an inmate to quit feeling angry and sorry for himself and to focus on bigger issues, you have done him a tremendous favor. I saw countless instances where something as simple as dropping the word "fuck" from a man's vocabulary, with all of its anger and negativity, radically changed his prison life. And I must say that the men who carried their Christian attitude back into the general population each day had a highly positive effect on that population. There was a lot of quiet mission work done. Not proselytizing, but counseling and comforting

36

"TURN OUT THE LIGHTS, THE PARTY'S OVER!"

I had surrendered to custody at the King County Jail on November 2, 1998. I spent one night there, then rode the Chain to The Washington Corrections at Shelton, Washington, where I stayed for six weeks. After processing there, I rode the Chain again to the Olympic Corrections Center at the northwest tip of the United States. I lived at OCC for twenty months. Finally, at the end of July, 2000, I was transferred to the Honor Farm at the Washington State Reformatory at Monroe, via two more Chain trips. My wrists were getting toughened up from the cuffs.

I spent a little more than a year at the Farm, officially named Monroe Correctional Center, Minimum Security Center (MCC-MSC), herding cows and selling milk. Finally, the day came when I was to be transferred to approximately six months of Work Release. Not absolute freedom, but it seemed like an enormous step toward absolute freedom.

There were many things to be done in order to get ready to end my prison life. I wanted to pass on the electric typewriter which I had acquired by clandestine means. When I got it in trade for a bunch of Store purchases, some buddies in the Property Room made it suddenly appear on my property records, as if I had brought it from OCC. That took some more Store purchases. The typewriter purchase had been of great benefit to my legal clients. I cranked out hundreds of pages of paperwork for inmate appeals and petitions, with a fair record of success. I didn't want any thing for the typewriter, but getting it off my property record and onto the new owner's was important. I chose a deserving inmate and simply carried it over to his house. The guys in the Property Room went to work again. The criminal mind is a wonderful and resourceful thing when employed in a good cause.

I was allowed to box up my personal items, which was a much bigger load than the first time I was transferred with my brown paper bag of belongings. Over three years, I had acquired a lot of books and clothing. I sent most of it out by mail, but took the bare essentials of clothing with me. I knew that I would be allowed to receive and buy cloths while I was at Work Release. I turned in all of my State Issue and gave up the ID badge that I had worn every instant for three years. For weeks I would slap at my chest when I felt my badge missing.

When the time came, five of us, in our own civilian clothes, climbed into a van. No cuffs! No chains! We just rolled down the highway like human beings and drove up in front of the Bishop Lewis House a few blocks uphill from downtown Seattle. The facility is an old 15-bedroom building which held about thirty work release inmates, each of whom would live there for the final six months or so of his sentence. My departure from Monroe had been delayed a month due to the lack of an opening at Bishop Lewis, so I would spend only five months there.

Bishop Lewis was privately operated by a company which benefited from the supply of low cost labor, much of which they employed in their own businesses at $8.00 per hour, with no benefits except room and board. It seemed to balance out for them. The staff was easy going non-cop civilians, but the rules were strict, and punishment for violations, particular the use of alcohol or drugs, was swift and sure. Occasionally we would all be confined to our rooms while some deputy sheriffs cam in from the King County Jail, a few blocks away, to haul away a violator.

I was assigned to a two-man room with a high ceiling and a bit of a view of the city. My cellie—or roomie now—was Marshall, a nice black man who I had known at OCC. He had lucked out in getting an excellent job in a bakery at $12.00 an hour.

Three hours after our arrival, we were given an "advance" check for $60.00 from the State of Washington, with an identification letter, since we had no ID. We were released—to the Streets!—for three hours to cash the check at Bank of America and to buy to toiletries at a store of our choosing.

I walked three blocks into downtown Seattle and was in shock. Pedestrian crosswalks through busy traffic frightened me. The idea that I was walking around in public without supervision was very troubling, and of course I thought that everyone was looking at me. Whenever a large passenger airplane passed overhead by the tall buildings, I was even more disturbed, as this was only a week after September 11, when I had watched the second suicide crash at the World Trade Center live on television. I had no confidence or swagger, and in fact was glad to be back in confinement in only two hours. I did not savor my time in freedom. This was going to take a while. I gained some understanding of long-term prisoners who offend again to get back into the comfort and security of imprisonment.

The glory of Work Release was that after we got a job and spent a couple of weeks in the facility, we were permitted to leave for a few hours at a time with approved persons. I got Mavis on my list and we were able to go out for dinner a couple times a week. I was not permitted to drink, and I had to watch her drink wine at dinner. It was not hard, as I had been dry for three years. As an additional incentive to sobriety, I knew that I would be given a UA upon my return to Bishop Lewis, and if I rang the bell I would be in the county jail the next day and on my way back to Shelton. That's incentive!

I had more UAs at Bishop Lewis than in my three previous years in confinement. I stayed clean.

The effect of three years of dryness was brought to me the day of my final release. Mavis' son had saved a bottle of fine champagne for a celebration. I had one glass and almost fell over. I regained my capacity before long.

My Five Years of Bad Coffee had ended! I was back in Seattle, the coffee capitol of the universe. In the early mornings when I walked downtown to catch the bus to work, I stopped in a Starbucks that was run by a friend of my daughter, and drank comp coffee. I had never been a big Starbucks fan, but I'm here to tell you their coffee is better than prison coffee.

My friend Glen hired me to work in his auction business, where I had worked before I went to prison. The job was located in South Seattle. I had to leave Bishop Lewis House at 6:00 in the morning and walk into downtown Seattle to catch a bus headed south. The town has a much different look and feel in the darkness of early morning than it does in the afternoons and evenings that I was more acquainted with. The sin of nighttime is dying out and the industry of daytime is beginning. Twice I ran into old Mexican friends from stir who appeared to have returned to their heroin dealing professions. They were courteous and clean to me and did not flaunt their pastime, but you can tell. What in hell is someone doing on the street at 6:00 a.m., obviously having been up all night, if he isn't selling heroin?

The months droned on. I became accustomed to the world, which is one of the purposes of Work Release. I got permission to go to choir practice in my old church, which was a twenty-minute walk from Bishop Lewis House, and I sang in the choir on Sundays. The Sunday schedule was sometimes pretty tight. The service began at 10:45 a.m., and I was expected back at 1:00 p.m. That seems a reasonable time frame if your church experience is limited to white churches. A

Caucasian minister reliably gets you out in 60 minutes or less. But black preachers can get wound up, and the services often run from two and a half to three hours. I sometimes had to sneak out the back of the choir loft when I saw my deadline coming up.

I cheated a bit. Some mornings instead of taking the bus south to my job I took it north to my home, where I picked up my little red pickup truck and drove it to work. A reunion with an old lover! On my way to work, I drove the truck to a Seattle's Best coffee shop in West Seattle, where I feasted on wonderful coffee and fresh coffee cake and read the New York Times. Heaven!

◆　　　◆　　　◆

Finally, the Day came! After forty months of confinement, I was checked out to leave Work Release in an uncerimonial routine, and I walked out the door a free man. I had parked my truck a block away the night before, and I walked to it and drove back to pick up my stuff. I went home and unloaded my possessions into a house that didn't seem like home.

For some reason, I had to go to Ballard, a Scandinavian section in the northwest section of Seattle. As I drove down a street, I saw a neat little Lutheran church that I had passed by for years. I stopped my truck and got out, and walked into the church and asked the secretary in the church office if I could go into the sanctuary. She said "sure", and I went in and sat down in a rear pew. I spent about fifteen minutes reflecting an my new life and thanking God.

978-0-595-37326-0
0-595-37326-7